BETWEEN THE SAUCE, STARS, AND HEAVEN

A Memoir of Love, Loss, and the Tables That Raised Us

BY: LOU BASENESE, JR.

Dedication

"Laura - The Angel that God sent me."

For Laura

In this moment, I pause to honor and celebrate you, my miracle, my steady hand, and my greatest gift this side of heaven. You are the light that pierced the shadows, the gentle whisper that quelled the storms, and the devoted heart that breathed life into mine.

How can I ever express the profound gratitude that fills my soul? You didn't just save my life. You gave it back to me, piece by piece, with your boundless grace, steadfast determination, and undying love.

Through every page of this book, may you feel the echoes of our journey together, the trials we've overcome, the laughter we've shared, and the moments that have forever shaped us. May these words serve as a testament to the unparalleled beauty of a love that knows no bounds.

With every fiber of my being, I dedicate this work to you, Laura, my partner, champion, and guiding star. May the world see what I see in you in these pages: the boundless strength and the radiant light that illuminates our path.

To you, always,

Louie

Acknowledgments

"In Appreciation: To Those Who Helped Along the Way"

The journey of creating this book has been both humbling and transformative, shaped at every turn by the support, encouragement, and generosity of others. This work could not have come into being without the contributions, large and small, of a deeply cherished circle of individuals. To all of you who helped breathe life into this vision, I offer my deepest and most enduring thanks.

To my trusted beta readers and critique partners Ruth Ward, Eila Ulyett, Max Basenese, Gayle Pierson, and Dayle Pierson, thank you for your thoughtful feedback, your honest insights, and your unwavering belief in the heart of this story. Your willingness to engage with this work so openly and critically has profoundly shaped the book it became.

With deepest gratitude, I acknowledge the extraordinary individuals whose courage, clarity, and refusal to give up saved my life during a sudden cardiac arrest. Peter Algazi, Megan Bright, and Geoff Dunlevie responded without hesitation, administering CPR and standing firm in the face of crisis. Kat Serano, the 911 dispatcher, stayed calm and focused, guiding the rescue efforts with precision. And Fire Captain Glenn White made a life-altering decision when he refused to pronounce me dead. Alongside Laura's unshakable presence, these five became instruments of grace in a moment when every second mattered. I am here because they believed, acted, and refused to let go. Their names are etched into the fabric of my life and my family's forever. To my dear friends and family, especially my loving wife Laura, Ruth Ward, and my son Lou III, your love, patience, and faith have been the foundation on which I stood during the many highs and lows of writing and self-publishing. Your presence reminded me, time and again, that I was never alone in this process.

To the mentors who have guided me with clarity and purpose, Ed Nunnally, Tim Celek, Dale Ward, and Andy Reinstra, thank you for offering your wisdom so freely and your encouragement so steadily. Your mentorship did more than guide my writing; it helped me navigate the inner journey that this memoir demanded. Your words lit the path forward when the road felt unclear.

To the memory of my late uncles, Gus Rampone and Vincent "Harvey" Togno, your lives and legacies shaped the spirit of this book. You taught me the meaning of perseverance, character, and quiet strength. Your stories live on in these pages, woven into the very fabric of what this book seeks to preserve. It has been an honor to share even a glimpse of the men you were.

And to you, the reader, thank you for choosing to spend time with this story. Whether you came to it through family ties, shared heritage, or curiosity, your presence means more than words can express. I hope that within these pages, you find something that resonates, inspires, or reminds you of your own story's worth.

To every person who offered time, encouragement, advice, or simply stood beside me as this book took shape, please know your role has not gone unnoticed. Your support is a lasting part of this work, and I carry that gratitude with me, always.

Thank you, from the bottom of my heart, for being part of this journey.

Foreword

"A Glimpse into the Story: Framing the Journey Ahead"

Thank you for picking up this book. As you turn these pages, I hope you open your heart to the lessons and moments that await discovery. This memoir serves as a poignant reminder of resilience, love, and quiet strength in a world full of surprises and challenges.

Let me start with a story from my own life. I still remember the day I thought I might break and how a single act of kindness taught me that hope can arrive in the smallest moments.

You will find moments that feel deeply personal but speak to us all. You will read stories of overcoming hardship, a celebration of faith, and an exploration of the strength we carry within.

May these words encourage you to walk your path with courage and grace. Let them spark fresh dreams, challenge old doubts, and renew your sense of purpose.

Here, you will see life's highs and lows laid bare, laughter beside sorrow, love beside loss, struggle beside redemption. Let these stories guide you, offering clarity and light for the future.

Above all, take your time with this book. Let it reach into the quiet corners of your heart, awaken your spirit, and touch something deeper within you.

I am honored to share this work and the transformation it offers. Thank you for joining me on this journey.

Warmest regards

Lou Basenese

Contents

Introduction

"Unveiling the Tapestry: An Introduction to the Tale"

Some moments in life carry a weight so rich that they seem to rise off the page, like the smell of sauce simmering on a Sunday afternoon, the quiet sway of a porch swing, or the sound of laughter echoing through streets that now live only in memory.

Netcong, New Jersey, cradled my childhood. It was a place where faith, family, and stubborn grit held everything together. Optimism wasn't something people talked about. It was baked into our way of life. No one stayed anonymous. We gathered for dinners that fed the soul as much as the stomach. And when it came down to what mattered, loyalty always won out over status or money.

This isn't just a book of stories. It's a patchwork stitched together from real lives: funny, messy, loving, and sometimes heartbreaking. There's an uncle whose mischief still makes us laugh, a father who showed rather than told what it means to serve, and a son whose presence lingers in ways that words can't always explain.

Something deeper holds it all together: a thread of connection that holds strong even when the world pulls at the seams. Faith shows up in unexpected places. Families fall apart and mend. Memories stick around, reshaping themselves into something that keeps us going.

Between the Sauce, Stars, and Heaven is my way of reaching back to honor the people and places that shaped me. And maybe, along the way, to shine a little light on the simple things that give life its deepest meaning.

So, sit down. The sauce is on, the stories are warm, and if you're still for a moment, you might just hear the stars humming in the background.

Prologue: The Day I Died

Triumph Over the Impossible
"A Story of Resilience and Renewal"

I was twenty days shy of my fifty-seventh birthday when everything changed. It was July 6, 2006. The sunbaked Newport Beach, California, and my wife and I stood at the water's rim, blissfully unaware that life was about to slip through my fingers. My heart gave out without warning. In a heartbeat, I was gone, no pulse, breath, or movement for twelve seconds multiplied by sixty.

Time stretched into silence. Waves lapped the shore as though nothing had shifted. The sky leaned toward dusk, bathing the sand in molten gold. As I teetered on the edge of existence for twelve heart-wrenching minutes, my wife's instincts surged to the forefront. Driven by a potent mixture of adrenaline and resolve, she applied life-saving techniques, battling the crippling terror and helplessness that sought to overpower her.

In that stillness, dreams did not flit before me, and no grand light called my name. Instead, I felt warmth, a gentle peace, a presence pulsing in the gap between heartbeats. It was as if the sauce of memory, the glitter of stars, and the whisper of heaven folded all at once into that breathless moment.

Then came my grandmother's voice, vivid as ever: "Cena, vieni a mangiare! è ora di cena!" Her words tumbled through me: supper, not dinner, whether in life or the afterlife, I couldn't tell. I heard dishes clatter, wine glasses sing, and the hum of our family's laughter.

Uncle Angelo's raucous cackle rose above it all, that gleam in his eye promising mischief and the next great tale. And suddenly, my chest heaved. I drew breath, felt my pulse return, and the world snapped back into focus.

The doctors called it a miracle. I call it a second chance.

I saw my grandfather sipping his homemade wine back on his porch in that paint-chipped rocking chair. The scent of grapevines and garlic cooking in olive oil with fresh basil clung to the air like incense.

I saw my father and mother, still young and dressed to the nines, dancing in the kitchen. My boisterous and stubborn uncles leaned over the table with riveting stories tucked in their pockets. And I saw myself a little boy again in Netcong, our town of Italian names and familiar faces, the kind of place where your barber knew your business and your priest knew your sins before you ever spoke them.

Then it hit me, not the pain in my chest or the shock of defibrillators, but the clear knowing that I had been part of something rare, A world fading one Sunday at a time. If I didn't write it down, it would slip away forever.

I came back with more than just a repaired heart; I came back with a mission.

This is *Between the Sauce, Stars and Heaven*, a love letter to the life that made me. It's about family, the kind that yells, screams, and hugs in the same breath while they shove a plate of spaghetti your way. It's about food for nourishment, identity, ritual, and connection. It's about Netcong, where garlic filled the air on Sundays, and Mass ended with macaroni and wine made in the basement.

And it's about characters. My God, we had characters, especially Uncle Angelo. Every great story needs a rogue, and he was ours. So, before this tale of town culture and family built one porch, one garden, one meatball at a time unfolds, I want you to meet him.

This is the story of a town, a family, and an uncle who painted our world with life, love, and a lot of sauce.

Chapter One

Uncle Angelo
"The Rogue in the Room"

"The Thrilling Dance of Mischief and Charm"

A Tale of Two Brothers
"The Porch Pickpocket"

Uncle Angelo

It was one of those summer evenings when the sky turned honey-gold, and the air smelled of garlic and warm pavement. Dad and I sat on the porch talking slowly while the ice cream truck's tune drifted down the block, and the vegetable man shouted; "Watermelon, lettuce, and peppers," as he pushed his cart.

That's when we spotted Angelo striding up the street. Dad leaned forward and let out a long sigh that told me trouble was coming. He muttered, "I know what he wants, but not tonight," as Angelo's car rolled to a stop, half on the curb.

Angelo climbed out with that familiar grin; eyes bright with mischief. Dad straightened and called out; "Don't come any closer, Angelo. I'm not giving you a cent, niente, nothing!"

Angelo shrugged as if he hadn't crossed a line and said, "All I want is to see my brother and nephew," before he stepped onto the porch.

They embraced in that brotherly way that melted stubbornness away. Dad's shoulders relaxed, and the night felt warm and safe again for a moment.

Throughout, Uncle Angelo's laughter echoed across the porch, promising that tonight's story had only just begun.

So, there we were the three of us, sitting on the porch as the sun dipped below the horizon. We told stories, laughed, and reminisced about the old days. Dad poured each of us a little wine, and we passed the bottle around, recalling Mama's cooking, the Yankees, and Grandpa's stubborn fig tree that hadn't fruited in years.

When it was time for Angelo to leave, he stood up, brushed off his slacks, and turned away with a casual, "Well, I gotta go." He walked a few steps, turned around, pulled something from his pocket, and tossed it back to Dad.

It was Dad's wallet.

"Thanks, brother," Angelo said with a wink, his walk turning into a trot. "I love you."

Dad instinctively opened his wallet, almost as if he needed to ensure it was real. And sure enough, it was but his wad of cash was $500 lighter, thanks to Angelo's lightning-fast maneuver.

Dad paused, sighed, and then turned to me with laughter in his eyes.

"That's Angelo for you," he said, shaking his head.

That was our Uncle Angelo. He didn't steal. He borrowed, he lifted, and he rearranged the flow of cash. Always with love, always with flair, and always, always with a punchline that left us in stitches. And that's how we knew, no matter what, that we were family.

Through laughter and sighs, we watched Angelo disappear into the night, his swagger as memorable as the stories he left behind. The gentle hum of cicadas filled the air, a reminder that time moved on, but the memories we shared would remain forever etched in the golden light of that summer evening. As Dad and I sat there on the porch, we knew we wouldn't have it any other way because family was everything, and love was the glue that held us together.

The Imperial Caper: A Tale of Brothers
"A Stubborn Car"

My father was a General Motors man through and through. Buick, Cadillac, Oldsmobile, and Pontiac were symbols of American ingenuity, their wide grilles and chrome fenders glinting with a promise of power and possibility. Yet in 1968, he broke tradition and brought home a Chrysler

Imperial. Perhaps it was the salesman's pitch, the price, or a fleeting moment of rebellion in the dealership lot. Whatever the reason, regret set in after a week, heavy and unrelenting, louder than the car's rumbling engine.

"I can't stand the damn thing," Dad muttered as he paced the driveway, glaring at the Imperial as though it had insulted our ancestors. He begged me to take it off his hands, but I refused, unsure what to make of this new family member. Attempts to sell the car failed; not even his brother Patsy, our resident used-car dealer, could help. With a sympathetic shrug, Patsy said, "Louie, some mistakes you just have to live with."

Left with no other options, Dad made the call you only place when you need something handled creatively. He called Uncle Angelo. I was there when Dad dialed him, and I can still hear the desperation in his voice as he asked for "a little help." True to form, Angelo agreed without hesitation.

"Louie," Angelo said, "just park the car in the driveway. Keys under the mat. Midnight. When you wake up tomorrow it will be gone, just like yesterday's news."

Dad followed those instructions as if they were gospel. Night after night, the Imperial sat in our driveway like a trophy no one wanted. For ten nights straight, Angelo stayed silent, and Dad's frustration grew. Every attempt to reach him met only radio silence, which was not surprising given Angelo's life as part "fixer" and philosopher.

Finally, on the eleventh day, Angelo picked up the phone. I still hear Dad roaring into the phone. "Where the hell have you been????" "I did everything you said, and that car is still in my driveway... You promised it would vanish."

Angelo let the storm pass. Then, in that calm drawl we knew so well, he said, "Louie I've been by your house all ten nights. The problem is your wife, Eva. She's been in that car every single night. She figured it out and she's not letting it happen."

Silence followed. Dad slammed down the receiver without another word to Mom. The next day, he traded the Imperial for a Cadillac and never mentioned it again. Angelo never crowed or pointed fingers. He shrugged and said, "Louie, you tried, I tried, and in the end, she won."

That was life with Dad, Angelo, and the rest of us: a chain of stories stitched together by laughter, frustration, and fierce love. The make or model of the car didn't matter. What mattered was the ride we shared and the bond we built along the way.

The Wild Ride to Vegas
"Paulie's Escape and Aunt Anna's Wrath"

In our family, time wasn't marked by clocks or seasons but by the stories that landed on our doorstep. On one warm afternoon in Netcong, we were all hanging on the corner, sharing jokes and that itchy sense of invincibility only teenage boys know.

Then Angelo's car rolled up, slowing to a deliberate stop. Paulie, Angelo's favorite project and Aunt Anna's son, strolled over, half curious, half afraid. "Where you headed, Uncle Ang?" he asked, voice tight. Angelo flashed that effortless grin and said, "Coffee. Just you and me. Get in."

We shrugged and watched Paulie climb inside. Just like that, they vanished without a wave or a goodbye, as if pulled into thin air.

The next morning, Aunt Anna unleashed hell. She was four-foot-six on a good day but carried herself like a general. Her voice cut through Netcong's streets, rattling screen doors and turning heads. She didn't need a backup. Her fury cleared sidewalks faster than any police cruiser.

She stormed every block, roaring Paulie's name, her eyes sharper than a rattlesnake's strike. Nobody crossed Aunt Anna. Her loyalty burned hotter than wrath, and when she came for you, you knew it meant business.

Stories like this stitched our lives together: wild rides, narrow escapes, fierce love, and ferocious protection. Through it all, we learned that family stories aren't just told but lived.

In the face of adversity, Aunt Anna's resolve never wavered. She paced the living room, promising pain for anyone who crossed her and vowing prayers for her family all at once. One minute, she'd threaten to break Angelo's kneecaps. Next, she'd light candles for his soul. Her heart burned hotter than any outrage yet beat with a fierce devotion that held us upright when the world whittled away at our hopes.

Folded arms and that trademark glare made her the sentinel who guarded our Land. Despite her diminutive size, Aunt Anna commanded the room with the undeniable presence of a seasoned general, her strong spirit compensating for her small physical stature. When she walked into a room, it felt like thunder rolling over hills. She was proof that fire doesn't need size to scorch.

Aunt Anna was the force that bound us together. She'd brave the fiercest storms for us and chastise angels should they dare go astray. A protector and a warrior, she embodied the comfort and reassurance of a soft bedtime prayer. With every shout, she forged a shield, and with every hug, she planted roots deep in our hearts.

Just as Netcong held its breath under her wrath, Paulie slipped back home. It was past midnight, and the house lay quiet. He tiptoed down the hallway, hoping to slip into bed without rousing the storm. But before he reached his door, the hallway light flared on.

There stood Aunt Anna, arms crossed, her silhouette carved by that single bulb. Her eyes cut through the darkness like blades. "Where have you been?" she demanded, her voice sharp enough to cut steel.

Paulie trembled as if caught in a gale. "Ma, I swear we just went for coffee and it turned into something else." He swallowed hard and met her gaze.

Aunt Anna's stare never wavered. "Where did you go for coffee?" she pressed.

And in that moment, Paulie knew Aunt Anna held every answer in her hands.

"We went to Vegas," Paulie confessed, bracing himself for what came next.

The events that unfolded next remain shrouded in uncertainty, leaving everyone to wonder and speculate about the truth. Rumors of yelling, wild hand gestures, and even a wooden spoon flashed through Netcong faster than any headline. One thing became clear: Paulie never disobeyed his mother again without a passport and a priest.

Angelo didn't stay hidden for long. Two weeks later, he reappeared on our block, his crooked grin and swagger intact. When someone asked why he'd whisk a teenager across the country without a word to Mom, he shrugged as if it were nothing. "The kid needed to learn about life. I gave him a real education."

No one argued. In our family, lessons came from wild rides and unforgettable characters, not textbooks. Stories like this were passed from one generation to the next, keeping

Angelo's mischief and Paulie's surprise alive long after the night ended.

Through it all, we learned that family means blood and stories that shared adventures bind us tighter than any promise ever could.

Angelo's Thanksgiving Fable
"The Creamo's Confession, A Rogue's Tale"

Thanksgiving Eve crackled with our old traditions of laughter, turkey roasting, and the buzz of excitement for what was to come after dinner. By eleven, Creamo's, the local bowling alley, transformed into a disco paradise. Under that glittering mirror ball, the Bee Gees replaced the crash of pins, and every face under thirty packed the floor.

I waited on the corner when Angelo's car glided up. His window rolled down, and there was that crooked smirk. "Where you headed tonight nephew," he asked, eyes dancing.

"Creamo's," I said, my voice full of promise. "Disco night."

He leaned in, as if about to share the world's best secret, and said, "Enjoy it; it won't be there after tonight."

I laughed; certain he was spinning another tall tale. "What do you mean?"

He dropped his voice low, "I've been hired to burn it down after they lock up."

His grin was impossible to read. Story or not, we piled into Creamo's, and it was everything we dreamed of: crowds pulsing, lights flashing, and music stuck in our bones. We danced, we flirted, and we felt like we owned the night.

Nobody wanted that feeling to end. Around two, the lights came up, and the crowd thinned. We slipped into the chill air outside, breathing hard and grinning. Creamo's was still there, safe and sound, under our feet.

As the cool air enveloped us, Angelo's voice echoed in my mind, an unmistakable reminder: "Remember what I told you." I couldn't help but feel a mix of surprise and amusement, realizing Creamo's still stood after our unforgettable night.

While the events of that fateful night were yet to unfold, the mythical aura surrounding Angelo's Thanksgiving Fable only grew stronger, etching itself deeper into our town's vibrant tapestry of legends.

The next morning, the smell of roasting turkey pulled me from sleep. I brushed aside the covers and wandered into the kitchen, where the radio blared the startling headline, "Creamo's burned." Laughter caught in my throat as Angelo's warning replayed that the rogue's tale had come true.

That evening, I found myself in my girlfriend's family kitchen. Leftovers sizzled on the stove, and her uncle, the local police chief, paced like he was chasing ghosts. He slammed his hand on the counter and thundered; "It was arson! I know it was arson!"

I held my breath and asked as innocently as I could; "How do you know for sure?

He stopped mid-stride and glared at me. "The building was ablaze in every corner when we arrived!"

I nodded and offered my girlfriend's mother a dish while tucking away that confession like a prized ruby. "Uncle Angelo, I thought, Uncle Angelo."

Angelo always filled a room long before he walked in. His laughter and grin cut through any silence, and if he hugged you, you might find your pockets mysteriously lighter.

And just like that, Angelo's legend grew another chapter. Creamo's was ashes, but his story kept burning bright in Netcong's memory.

Reflection

These stories made us laugh and still do, but they carry deeper shades when you grasp the world from which Angelo and my father came. Family tales recount how Angelo, at 10 years old, skillfully navigated playground disputes like a young "fixer," mastering the art of negotiation and problem-solving long before he learned fractions. Their childhoods were marked by the weight of poverty that settled into their bones. They swapped textbooks for toolboxes and lunch lines for loading docks. Most brothers quit school far too early, forced into an adult world before their legs steadied. They never dreamed of abstract success, only of dinner on the table, shoes without holes, and a warm home when winter's cold set in.

That upbringing shaped each of them in its way. Some hardened against the world. Others softened with quiet hope. But Angelo caught fire. He lived at full throttle, his laughter booming, always racing ahead of the pack.

Uncle Angelo wasn't a black sheep. He was our spark. While the rest of us orbited safe routines, he jumped the fence of expectation, lighting up every room he entered. He broke the rules the way some broke bread, unapologetic, generous, and unforgettable.

The memories remain vivid: the laughter, the mischief, and the tall tales, reminders of a man who refused to be boxed in by circumstance. Angelo's stories, embroidered with just enough truth to sting, wove themselves into our family's fabric, proof that life's most unpredictable moments become its richest legends.

Maybe Angelo sensed he'd never grow old. He moved through life with the urgency of a man pressed for time. And perhaps that's why, at thirty-eight, he left us struck down by a virus he contracted during his military service, a silent invader that quietly took hold of his heart and never let go. Over the years, it wore him down from the inside out, damaging the same heart that once beat with purpose, pride, and just enough mischief to slip out past curfew, charm the cops, and stroll in the next morning like nothing ever happened. In the end, that wild, wonderful heart simply finally came to rest.

His passing came too soon, yet it matched the rhythm of his life. He always lived to the fast beat of a clock ticking louder than anyone else's.

In the quiet that followed his death, we learned one final lesson: that to live boldly, without apology or regret, is the greatest gift one life can offer another. And in that, Angelo remains alive in us all.

He laughed until his sides ached, schemed bolder than any of us dreamed, and loved with a force that carved its memory into our hearts. Angelo gave us something rare for all the chaos he left behind: stories that stuck like seeds, sprouting laughter years later. He painted our black-and-white world boldly, proving life was more than bills and survival. Life was about seizing moments, embracing risk, and laughing so fiercely that it made you forget how hard everything once was.

Angelo's life may have been brief, but it burned bright. He refused to let circumstance write his story, living with bold strokes and an unapologetic style. His tales wove into every family gathering, a reminder that reality's best lines often come from the rogue at the table.

Whenever Angelo entered a room, you felt it, whether you welcomed him or bristled at the uproar. And when he left, you talked about him in hushed tones, eager to relive every outrageous detail. Even now, as I sit with these memories, I can't help but grin at the rogue who bumped my elbow with a wink and lightened my pockets with a laugh.

Angelo didn't wear a cape; he chose a leather jacket that carried too much cash and made Imperials vanish on a dare. He broke the rules not out of malice but for the thrill of living on the edge. And always, he showed up ready to spark a story or mend a heart.

His laughter still echoes in our kitchens, his swagger in our doorways, and his mischief in every whispered family legend. Life taught us, through its wild rides, that the richest lessons are found away from textbooks, instead in moments you never saw coming.

Here's to Angelo, the uncle who lived fully, loved fiercely, and laughed often. He proved that heroes don't need capes, just courage, a crooked grin, and an unquenchable spark. Tonight, we raise a glass for the rogue in the room for the spark that lit up our world, and for every memory he left blazing bright.

Chapter Two

Netcong

"The Town That Raised Us"

"A Tale of Growth and Belonging"

You could smell Sunday from a block away. Garlic sizzling in olive oil drifted through the streets like a hymn, and somewhere, Sinatra crooned as if it were scripture. Before the bells rang at St Michael's, families were dressed, men in short sleeves and aftershave, women in heels and hope. Faith was not optional. It flowed through every porch conversation and kitchen prayer in Netcong, the little town that raised us.

Netcong felt mighty despite its size, like a village carved from old stone and stubborn will. We didn't just know our neighbors; they raised us. Italian immigrants and their American-born children-built lives with grit, not gold. The porch became a gathering place, and yards were transformed into vineyards. Tomato plants stood guard along fences like silent battalions. Even the air had an accent.

Our parents spoke Italian, and our grandparents swore in it, but we weren't allowed to. We spoke English. We were Americans. That rule wasn't just spoken. It was lived. Still, we carried Italy in our marrow in the way we cooked our Sunday sauce and in the hand gestures that punctuated every story.

From those narrow streets and crowded kitchens came police chiefs, educators, business owners, war veterans, and mentors, men and women who saw hard work not as a burden but as a badge. They learned early that gratitude was the currency that never lost value.

I remember trudging to school in winter, the cold biting through our jackets, yet none of us complained. Complaints were wasted breath. Our fathers labored in factories and on construction sites, and our mothers' scrubbed floors and raised children while pinching every penny. We learned that life's difficulties were meant to be met head-on and that family would always catch you if you fell.

Tragedy wasn't rare. We lost aunts and uncles almost every summer, and somehow, those losses made our laughter louder and our faith not just a ritual but a survival skill. Through it all, Netcong shaped us. It taught us that belonging meant more than sharing a street name. It meant sharing a purpose and a promise to stand by each other no matter what.

In Netcong, we found who we were and who we were meant to become. Every time I smell garlic on a Sunday; I'm reminded that home isn't just a place. It's the people and the stories that carry us through.

My father was one of eleven children, nine brothers and two sisters, and my mother came from a family of seven, four brothers and three sisters. Our house was always overflowing, even when no one knocked on the door. Uncles dropped in unannounced, aunts delivered pastries wrapped in paper, and cousins felt more like siblings than distant relatives. The line between immediate and extended family became completely blurred. You belonged if you shared a last name or a tip on how to fold laundry.

Every aunt and uncle contributed something unique to our family table: food and character. Some were the quiet backbone, steady and sure, without needing the spotlight. Others held court as storytellers and jokers. A few served as disciplinarians or dancers. Some were war veterans, others ran small businesses, and a couple you never dared to question too closely. Together, they shaped every version of who we became.

The aunts held the family's soul. Fierce and tender, opinionated yet tireless, they cooked with heart and corrected with a single look. They preserved traditions of meatball making and sauce stirring and taught girls and boys what strength looks like, worn under an apron and spoken with conviction.

We learned early that family was more than birthright. It was a fortress to defend. Arguments erupted, sometimes over cards, other times over whose sauce reigned supreme, but always beneath the clash lay an unbreakable code: we protected our own.

We carried that code into pride, proud to trace our roots to Italy but prouder still to call ourselves American. Patriotism for us sprang from memory and sacrifice rather than politics. Our flags flew on the Fourth of July, yet every day, we honored the chance our parents and grandparents seized when they left their homeland behind. That pride showed in how we stood for the anthem with our right hand over our heart, dressed for church, and worked each day as if we owed the land we lived on our best effort.

In Netcong, we weren't just neighbors; we were a family forged by shared struggle and bound by stories. Every time I step through a doorway into a bustling kitchen, I'm reminded that home is where the heart of many beats as one.

When I look back now, I see that Netcong was more than a hometown. It was a proving ground, a place that forged our identity, shaping who we were and who we would become. It turned immigrant children into citizens, contributors, and leaders. It taught us that legacy isn't just what you inherit. It's what you pass on.

And while the streets have changed, and many of the porches we sat on now sit quiet, the town still lives in me. It lives in the way I shake hands, in how I run my business, in how I raise my children. It lives in the ache I feel every time I remember a cousin's laugh, an aunt's voice, a Sunday table that no longer exists.

The town that raised us didn't just raise a generation. It built a legacy.

Reflection

Looking back, I now understand that Netcong wasn't just where we lived but where we became. The soil was humble, the streets were narrow, and that small town gave rise to lives of enormous purpose. It taught us that legacy isn't about monuments. It's about memory, meaning, and how a place shapes your bones without you even realizing it. Netcong gave us more than stories. It gave us a compass, always pointing us in the right direction. And long after we left, that compass kept pointing home.

Netcong wasn't just an address. It was a training ground for everything that was to come next. A little place tucked into the hills of northwest New Jersey, where everyone knew everyone, and nearly every last name ended in a vowel. Your grandparents might've lived two blocks over, your cousin next door, and your first crush probably became your prom date. There was only one main street, and you couldn't walk without someone leaning out of a storefront to say hello or tell your mother where they saw you last.

Church bells from St. Michael's set the rhythm of our days. Everything from Friday fish-only dinners to First Communions started and ended there. The school, the park, Direnzo's, the corner store with penny candy, and DelVeccio's Market, where Oglie and Mary made the best Italian subs on fresh bread, were our landmarks. It wasn't flashy, but it was home.

The town was built by immigrants and held together by their children and grandchildren. Netcong was split by railroad tracks, literally. Families from Naples, like mine, lived on one side of the track. On the other hand, families from Cesa, a town in the Campania region, whom we called "Chez, " lived on the other side. There was a friendly yet fierce rivalry between the two sides, and each summer, that rivalry came to life through a sacred tradition.

The Chez families celebrated the Feast of St. Cesario in late July, while the Naples side honored the Feast of the Assumption in mid-August. Both began with early morning Mass, followed by a six-hour procession through the streets of Netcong, each side carrying their patron saint high above the crowd. Italian grandmothers and mothers pinned money onto the saints as offerings. The procession paused often at homes where tables overflowed with food and drink, ancestors were honored, and neighbors were fed. Fireworks burst through the sky in memory, honoring the deceased with light and sound.

The day always ended with a full-blown Italian festival: food, music, raffles, rides, and the biggest fireworks show anyone could remember. It wasn't just a celebration. It was a homecoming for former residents, far-flung families, and curious visitors from all over the state. Even now, the tradition lives on a heartbeat echoing from the past, reminding us that no matter how far we've gone, we all came from the same feast.

Everyone had a garden. Everyone had a grapevine. And during harvest season, every garage smelled like wine in progress. You could tell what street you were on by the sauce in the air, some heavier on basil, some with more heat, some with a hint of sweetness. And if you happened to walk by at just the right time, you might get invited in for a taste.

A village raised us, and the village looked after its own. When someone died, the whole town mourned. When someone succeeded, the town rejoiced. There was no privacy, which was part of the charm. The walls were thin, the lives were loud, and the love was thick.

Netcong didn't just shape us; it gave us roots and wings. It was, in every sense, an incubator for success and significance in the lives of the children who grew up there. It was not the kind of place that made headlines, but the kind that made character. The potential wasn't cultivated in ivy-covered halls but nurtured in small kitchens, on church steps, and across backyard fences.

People learned how to work hard, show up, keep their word, and how and when to keep their mouths shut. It bred discipline in the boys and grace in the girls. Teachers didn't just educate, they mentored. Coaches didn't just teach the game. They taught life. And the church didn't just shape Sunday, it shaped our consciences

The entire community felt like one big, extended family in our beloved town of Netcong, New Jersey. At the heart of that family were our protectors, the Netcong Police Force.

The dynamic duo led this two-person team: Police Chief Marcellus "Mooch" De Muccio and Lieutenant Andy "G" Gugliemini. The idyllic scenes of Mayberry R.F.D. didn't come close to the warmth and camaraderie of our town.

Our police officers weren't just badge-wielding enforcers; they were neighbors, friends, and sometimes even disciplinarians. Take "Mooch," for instance. One look from him, and we knew we were in trouble. But his kind of justice always came with a dose of compassion the kind only someone who saw you like family could give.

If Mooch caught you red-handed, he didn't always slap you with a ticket or haul you in. More often, he'd march you straight to the last place you wanted to go: Home. Facing your parents was a punishment no citation could ever match.

One unforgettable incident involved a friend who got pulled over for driving under the influence. Mooch didn't impound the car. He didn't throw him in the back seat or haul him to the station. Instead, he locked up the vehicle, placed my staggering friend in front of his cruiser, and slowly followed him home. Stumbling along, my buddy approached the front porch, step by step, under Mooch's watchful eye. When they arrived, Mooch rang the bell and, with the seriousness of a judge handing down a sentence, announced: "Here's your son. I caught him driving intoxicated." He handed over the keys and walked off, knowing the real punishment was waiting inside.

So here's to Mooch, Andy "G," and the Netcong Police Force. They may not have had the fanciest badges or the sleekest squad cars, but they had something far more important: hearts of gold and a deep love for our town and its people. Their compassion and camaraderie made Netcong the quintessential small town where life was simple, laughter was plentiful, and everyone looked out for one another.

In Netcong, success wasn't always measured in money or titles but in how you carried yourself, how you treated others, and what you gave back. That's why many of us who grew up there became principals, industry captains, Fortune 500 executives, military officers, entrepreneurs, union leaders, clergy, and community icons. Netcong taught you how to be somebody, not by inflating your ego but by anchoring your values. It taught you that significance was earned, not given, and that true greatness often begins in humble places. It taught us that we make a living by what we get, money and material things, but making a life is all about giving.

A pillar of that learning came through the doors of Netcong High School, which operated from 1906 until its closure in 1974. At its peak, the entire student body hovered around 230 students, yet its impact on our town was immeasurable. The school was more than just a place of learning; it was the heartbeat of the community. Its football, basketball, and wrestling programs were followed with near-religious devotion. Each game or match was a modern-day David versus Goliath story, as our small team took on much larger schools and often emerged victorious. The stands were always full, and the town came alive in those moments with the unity only sports can provide.

We were lucky to have teachers who were more than educators. They were life mentors. Men like Gus Rampone, our algebra teacher and head football coach, taught us discipline with a bark and a wink. Vincent "Harvey" Togno, our PE and health education teacher who later became Superintendent, led with the strength and passion of a Marine Master Sergeant. And then there was Carmine "Mo" DeMuccio, who coached football and basketball and inspired generations of young men to believe in themselves, even when the odds weren't in their favor. These were not just authority figures; they were guides, shaping boys into men and teammates into brothers.

When the high school closed in 1974, something vital shifted. It was more than the loss of a building. It was the fraying of a communal thread. Many of us left town to pursue our dreams; over time, those tightly woven family units began to loosen. The rhythm of Sunday dinners faded. The gardens weren't planted as often. But the lessons remained. The memories lived on. And the roots, while stretched, never really left the soil of Netcong.

Main Street Netcong – Circa 1940

Main Street Netcong – The beating heart of my past

Feast of the Assumption – Netcong's display of faith

Mother Mary – Carried with devotion, a sacred procession

Netcong High School – A cornerstone of our community

Vincent "Harvey' Togno – Shaped us into men

Gus Rampone – Our team- His Battlefield

Carmine "Mo" DeMuccio
A Guiding Light

Netcong High School History

Chapter Three

Roots in the Old Country

"The Cradle of Our Family's Story"

Where the Story Truly Unfolds

Before our ancestors crossed the sea and faced Ellis Island, they lived under the harsh sun of southern Italy. In villages like Carpino, arid fields and twisting lanes shaped their spirit, faith, and grit. Time moved slowly there, and every day felt like a test of endurance.

Life in those towns was raw and unforgiving. Before dawn, the men rose to tend goats and vines. They pruned olive trees and turned the soil baked by the sun. Their hands bore the stains of long labor, and their shoulders carried the weight of family duty, centuries-old tradition, and poverty that clung tight.

The school was a luxury. Most boys swapped books for tools, and paperwork meant nothing besides calloused palms. Literacy was rare, but wisdom born of the land was everywhere.

Women kept the village's heart beating. They bore children without doctors, scrubbed laundry in icy basins, and made meals from scraps. Their strength matched the mountains, and their days were measured by planting seasons, harvests, feast days, and funerals.

That harsh beauty forged our ancestors' roots. They learned to pray at first light and celebrate under starlit skies. Faith and family flourished even when life offered little else.

In that rugged land, the Basenese legacy took hold. Long before any name was changed or a new life began across the ocean, our family learned what it meant to endure, to hope, and to carry that hope forward.

In this world, girls became wives before they had a chance to become women, and boys were thrust into manhood before they'd even tasted the sweet nectar of childhood innocence. Joy was not found in abundance but in the simple rituals that wove the fabric of their lives: the comforting aroma of stewing tomatoes, the hushed reverence of evening prayers, the fleeting enchantment of carnival, and the warmth of shared bread.

Modern conveniences like electricity and plumbing were, but distant dreams and medicine beyond folk remedies and fervent prayers were practically nonexistent. Death, a haunting specter, came early and often in the form of disease, famine, or despair. Yet, they persevered. What they lacked in material comfort, they more than made up for in spirit, in the sheer force of their will to carry on.

So, when a man like Gabriel, born in 1888, chose to leave this world behind, he wasn't merely escaping poverty; he was severing the chains of centuries-old inertia. He was risking everything on a future he couldn't see, in a language he couldn't speak, and with a name that no one would pronounce correctly. And behind him, a woman like Donata held the village together in his absence, helping her family raise children in the same aching soil. Eventually, she found the courage to brave the vast ocean herself.

This is where our story truly begins not in America, not at the dock, but in a humble stone house nestled in the shadows of the Apennines, where a mother's lips brushed her son's forehead in a tender farewell, and her whispered prayers begged the Madonna to return him to her safe and whole.

They were not myths, nor were they perfect. But they were survivors, unbreakable spirits, undying dreams echoing through generations to come. We, their descendants, are the living testament to their courage, strength, and indelible legacy.

Part I: The Journey and the Man (Gabriel)

As I close my eyes, I can almost feel the presence of my paternal grandfather beside me, his weathered hands a testament to the toil and grit of a life well-lived resting on his knees. Born on April 5, 1888, in Carpino, a small mountain town nestled within the province of Foggia, Italy, he was a man shaped by the rich scents of olives and the determined spirit of hard labor that permeated the very air he breathed. The pride and resilience of Carpino's people, their hands worn like leather gloves, were an enduring reminder of their dogged pursuit of survival.

In 1907, at the tender age of nineteen, my grandfather made the arduous and fateful decision to leave behind the only world he had ever known. Boarding the steamship Leon XIII with a mere $12 in his pocket, he set sail for America. Twelve dollars is a number that has resonated with me throughout my life, an emblem of faith, determination, and an unwavering belief in a brighter future not only for himself but for generations yet unborn, for a family name yet to make its mark in the land of opportunity.

His transatlantic voyage, far from the romanticized image often portrayed, was a grueling and unforgiving journey. As a third-class passenger, he found himself crammed into the dark and dank bowels of the ship known as steerage. Any semblance of privacy was non-existent. Rows upon rows of narrow bunks, lined with straw mattresses often damp and infested with lice, bore witness to the brutal reality of this passage. Toilets were scarce, and the stench of seasickness clung stubbornly to the air, a constant reminder of the hardships endured by all those who dared to dream.

Meager and unappetizing meals consisted of thin soup, hard bread, and perhaps some beans or salted meat. Yet, even these simple offerings were often too much for the churning seas to allow. The sounds of suffering filled the darkness;

babies cried, old men groaned, and women whispered fervent Hail Marys at all hours. Rosaries were clutched tightly not only as symbols of faith but also as talismans of sanity amidst the unrelenting turmoil.

As I sit with these memories, I can almost hear their whispered prayers rising from the bowels of the ship, faint but full of desperation and the steady, determined breath of the young man who would become my grandfather. Through the stench, the seasickness, the fear, and the relentless sway of uncertainty, he endured. The Atlantic may have tossed his body, but his spirit never wavered. He carried more than just hope. He carried a dream, heavy but alive, meant not only for himself but for all of us who would come after.

The first sighting of the Statue of Liberty must have felt like a miracle, a towering symbol promising a new life. But the journey wasn't over. Ellis Island still stood between him and the world he had risked everything to reach. The inspections that followed were swift and clinical, almost brutal in their cold efficiency. Doctors moved through the crowds, marking the sick with letters chalked onto coats: **E** for eye disease, **H** for heart trouble, and **X** for mental illness. For many, a single mark could mean the end of their American dream before it even began.

My grandfather made it through. Just barely. And with that passage, he began to lose the last fragments of the man he had been. Language, accents, unfamiliar ears—these turned Abriiele Baccanicco into someone new, again and again.

Abraham Basini. Gabriel Basaneso. Gabriel Basenese. Each name, each spelling, chipped away at what he had brought with him. In America, names weren't heirlooms. They were clay reshaped, erased, and rewritten by clerks, customs officers, by systems that couldn't, or wouldn't, understand.

Still, he didn't flinch. He didn't fight it. Maybe this was his silent way of stepping into a new life, not with resistance but with resolve. He gave up a name but claimed a future. And in doing so, he gave us ours.

He settled in Netcong, New Jersey, a small, predominantly White Anglo-Saxon Protestant town that would, over time, pulse with an Italian heartbeat as more immigrants like my grandfather planted their roots there. Netcong became more than a dot on a map. It became a beacon. A place where southern Italian dialects spilled from open windows, laundry lines fluttered like prayer flags above narrow yards, and the scent of Sunday sauce drifted from one home to the next, binding neighbors in a kind of unspoken communion.

In Netcong, front porches turned into confessionals, kitchen tables into councils. My grandfather, working long hours for meager wages, sometimes less than the minimum, still managed to save enough to buy a house. Not a grand estate, but a place he could truly call his own. With time, he added a panoramic porch, a small architectural triumph, and a quiet declaration: I'm not going anywhere. We came to call it "The Big House," and for over forty years, it stood as the beating heart of our family.

There, wine was bottled, and stories fermented alongside it. The sauce was stirred in cast iron pots seasoned with generations of memory. Babies were cradled, arguments sparked and fizzled, and holidays crowned the calendar like sacred rituals. That house wasn't just shelter; it was an heirloom made of wood, stone, and will.

Gabriel Basenese, a man who had crossed an ocean and surrendered pieces of his identity along the way, had finally found a home. Within those walls, wrapped in the scent of simmering tomatoes, the echo of laughter, and the rhythm of footsteps across old floors, the essence of who we are took root.

Perched on a gentle hill overlooking the calm, shimmering surface of Lake Musconetcong, "The Big House" wore its panoramic porch like a crown. It looked out onto a landscape stitched with vineyard rows, vegetable beds, and that glinting expanse of water that mirrored the sky. But it was what happened on that porch that mattered most.

It became our family's altar. Cousins became confidants there. News was delivered, decisions made, jokes told, and stories spun. Squabbles flared and faded before dinner was served. And in all of it, through the loud and the quiet, the messy and the magical, our family stitched itself together again and again.

Every Sunday, without fail, all eleven siblings arrived at "The Big House" with their spouses and children in tow. Cars lined the street like offerings at a sacred temple, and children spilled out into the yard, their laughter rising like music into the air. The porch buzzed with a melodic collision of Italian and English, a joyful chorus of greetings, teasing, and familiar retellings of family lore. Inside, the house pulsed with life, a whirlwind of clinking dishes, shouted names, shared memories, and the kind of love that doesn't need to be spoken to be understood. It was a weekly symphony of beautiful chaos, a perfectly imperfect ballet of familial devotion that spilled through doorways, danced down hallways, and breathed life into every wall of "The Big House."

The roots of that love were planted long before, in the lives of Louie and Eva, my parents, who carried forward the foundation of faith, perseverance, and sacrifice that my grandparents had so painstakingly laid. Their example, built on quiet strength and tireless resolve, shaped the moral compass of our family. That same spirit born in hardship and nurtured in love wound its way into the lives of their children and grandchildren, quietly guiding our steps through the decades. It helped us bridge the gap between two worlds: embracing the American dream without severing the sacred thread that tied us to our Italian heritage.

My grandfather's legacy, once a boy crossing the Atlantic in steerage with twelve dollars and a name that wouldn't survive immigration, blossomed in the laughter, stories, and sacred rituals of Sundays at "The Big House." That house became more than a home; it was a living archive of who we were and who we were becoming. In its rooms, traditions took root. Around its table, dreams were quietly nourished. And from its foundation, our family grew deeply connected to the soil of our past and ever-reaching toward the future we were still learning to create.

Part II: The Woman Who Held the World (Donata)

Donata, my grandmother, embarked on a journey not so different from that of my grandfather. In 1910, just a few years after him, she crossed the same vast, unforgiving ocean, carrying with her the same mixture of trepidation and hope that had fueled the dreams of countless immigrants before her.

Her voyage mirrored his in hardship, the same cramped quarters below deck, the same rough seas rocking the boat and stomach alike, the same tightly clutched suitcase holding not only her few possessions but the weight of an unknown future. Yet there was one stark difference: Donata arrived in America with her future already scripted. A prearranged marriage awaited her.

In those days, the notion of romance was a luxury they could not afford. Their union was not sparked by courtship or whimsy but anchored instead in duty, resilience, and faith. A promise made in a distant village by two families bound them together, and from that vow, a life was built. What followed was not the pursuit of personal dreams but the relentless labor of building a shared future, one that placed survival above sentiment, sacrifice above comfort, and legacy above fleeting desires.

The immigrant experience in early 20th-century New Jersey demanded a delicate balancing act between assimilation and identity, between honoring the old country and adapting to the new world. Italian immigrants, like my grandparents, often found solace in tight-knit enclaves where familiar dialects could still be spoken and where Catholic parishes functioned as both sacred havens and social lifelines. The church was more than a place of worship. It was a living, breathing epicenter of community life, where jobs were exchanged in hushed tones, names of potential landlords were whispered after Mass, and baptisms, funerals, and wedding announcements were tucked between scripture readings and rosaries.

The work available to them was arduous, often invisible, and always undervalued. My grandfather and his peers took on the jobs no one else wanted: construction, railroads, coal yards, and janitorial work labor that broke their backs but never their spirits. For every brick they laid and every track they nailed, they built something bigger than the structures around them. They built dignity, permanence, and the scaffolding of a future their children could climb.

Meanwhile, women like Donata anchored the home front with a quiet but immovable force. Beneath their soft voices and graceful movements was an unwavering strength. They were not simply wives and mothers. They were gardeners coaxing life from unfamiliar soil, bakers feeding entire families with their hands and hearts, and sewists who mended not just clothes but the frayed edges of immigrant life. They were the keepers of culture, tradition, and faith. With flour-dusted aprons and sun-worn hands, they raised more than just children; they raised communities, cultivated resilience, and instilled a sense of belonging that reached far beyond their front doors. Their labor, often unseen, was no less foundational, it was the heartbeat of a home, the root system of a legacy.

Discrimination shadowed their early years in America, harsh, unspoken, and sometimes emblazoned in cruel clarity on storefronts and factory gates: "No Italians Need Apply." Still, they endured. They adapted. And brick by metaphorical brick, they built something no prejudice could dismantle. What they lacked in formal opportunity, they made up for in relentless drive. They opened their shops, claimed narrow plots of land, and forged a future from the very soil that once seemed to reject them.

Their legacy wasn't passed down in dollars, deeds, or titles. It came instead as something quieter and far more lasting: an inherited fortitude. It seeped into the next generation by way of dinner table stories and unspoken lessons. You saw it in the way they rose before dawn, how they worked with their hands, how they bore difficulty with grace. My father and his siblings didn't grow up expecting comfort. They earned every inch of it. In their world, labor wasn't just a necessity; it was a virtue.

Whether in the garden rows, the basement workshops, or the frozen pipes, they learned to thaw with hot towels; they were taught to mend, to serve, to show up. Problems weren't pondered. They were met. If something broke, you fixed it. If someone bled, you ran to them. If a cousin needed a ride or a neighbor needed soup, the answer was always yes. There was no room for vanity and certainly no time for complaint. But pride, sacred pride, in their identity as Americans ran deep, even as they whispered prayers in Italian, fermented grapes in cellars, and hung laundry to dry while speaking the dialect of the old country across chain-link fences.

That same indomitable spirit, the one tempered by hardship, refined by self-denial, and burnished with faith, found its way into the hearts of Louie and Eva, my parents. The roots planted by those who came before them did not merely anchor. They pointed the way forward. Louie and Eva carried with them the resilience of their ancestors, using it as a lantern to light their American path. And in that glow, our family continued to grow. What was built in struggle became a framework of love, an architecture of values strong enough to carry generations. This legacy was and remains the quiet engine behind everything we are.

As our family walked the tightrope between honoring the traditions of the old world and embracing the promises of a new American identity, the legacy of Louie and Eva stood as our anchor. It reminded us not only of the sacrifices they had made but of the hope they planted, hope that would become part of the very fabric of our lives. Their choices didn't just shape their destinies; they laid the foundation for a lineage built on faith, endurance, and an abiding love that stretched across generations like an unbroken chain.

Through every trial and triumph that followed, the spirit of Louie and Eva endured rooted in the wisdom of their ancestors, nourished by the dream of a better tomorrow. That same spirit reached me like a whisper passed down through time, instilling within me the courage to walk my path, the strength to endure, and the grace to carry our family's story forward. In the stitching together of past and present, of tradition and transformation, the lives of my parents left an indelible mark, one that testifies to the enduring power of family, faith, and the pursuit of something greater than oneself.

This was the legacy that shaped those who came after them, a legacy not of wealth or privilege but of quiet strength, steadfast devotion, and the ability to find light in even the darkest hours. It taught us that hardship could be met without complaint, that laughter could be our balm, and that gratitude was a way of life, not just a passing sentiment. It shaped the way I see the world and, ultimately, became the foundation on which my own story was built.

The Basenese Brotherhood – Laughter and stories

A Circle of Grace – My Aunts – The heart of our family

Louie & Eva – United in love. Their story began here

Chapter Four

Louie and Eva

"The Enduring Influence - Love and Guidance"

That was the legacy that shaped the next generation, a legacy rooted in faith and family, in struggle borne without complaint, in laughter that softened the hardest days, and in gratitude that endured even in adversity. It was a foundation built of fire and devotion, and it took root deeply in Louie and Eva and, in time, in me.

It shaped my parents most profoundly. My father, one of eleven children, grew up in that same house with a panoramic porch, absorbing everything the immigrant experience had to teach: resilience, resourcefulness, and reverence for tradition. From a young age, he understood that family wasn't just a word. It was the first and last institution that mattered. His childhood was not marked by leisure but by labor and loyalty. Often, he set aside his schooling to help support the household, never seeking praise, never voicing complaints. He simply did what was needed because that's what love and duty looked like in his world.

Even before the world was at war, Louie understood service. At just seventeen, he enlisted in the U.S. Army not for glory or recognition but out of a quiet conviction passed down by his parents. He fulfilled his commitment with honor. But when World War II erupted, he answered again, this time with the Navy. He didn't do it for medals. He did it for the country he cherished, the family he longed to protect, and the deep, unshakable sense of responsibility he carried not on his sleeve but in his bones.

My mother, Eva, came from a family of seven, just a mile away, yet rooted in the same rich soil of tradition and grit. Her home was a sanctuary of closeness where siblings were second parents, and elders commanded reverence like saints. Dignity wasn't asked for; it was expected. Faith wasn't taught; it was lived. Pride in their Italian heritage was not something spoken it was evident in every gesture, every ritual, every shared meal.

Together, Louie and Eva didn't just carry the legacy forward; they carried it with honor, not as a burden but as a torch. In their hands, tradition was not something to be endured; it was something to be lived, passed on, and burned into the hearts of their children. And from their quiet strength and their unwavering guidance, a new chapter of our family's story began lit by the fire they kept alive.

Louie, my father, was the embodiment of the provider. In our household, he was the firm, unwavering figure, stern, unyielding, and utterly resolute in his discipline. He never entertained disobedience; the rules were clear, and they were meant to be followed. His strictness, however, was tempered by the immense sacrifices he made. Louie worked three jobs to keep the family afloat: a full-time butcher by day, a special police officer on weekends, and a night shift security guard at a dynamite plant. He wasn't a man of many words, but his actions were loud enough to speak for him. If anyone needed something, anything at all, Louie was the one you called.

To his siblings, Louie was a godfather figure. The fixer, the go-to person who had connections everywhere, from politicians to tradespeople, knew how to get things done. Beneath that powerful exterior, though, was a young boy who had to grow up too quickly, a boy who left school behind to support a family that struggled to survive. He never quite shook the feeling of not being good enough, and those insecurities, whether intentional or not, were passed down to me.

For much of my life, I sought his approval, even in moments when I should have sought peace. His presence loomed large, and I spent countless years trying to prove myself worthy of his standards, as though those achievements would finally earn me the approval I so deeply longed for. Even after his passing, I found myself reaching for his acknowledgment a futile pursuit at times when I should have focused on inner peace instead.

Eva, my mother, was the balance. Where Louie was fire, Eva was water. She softened his sharp edges with a grace that never faltered. She was our protector, stepping in when the weight of his sternness became too much for us to bear. Her gentleness didn't make her weak; it only made her more revered.

Both Louie and Eva were deeply faithful. Sunday Mass wasn't just a routine, it was a ritual, one that carried the reverence of tradition. And Sunday afternoons were sacred. Long lunches at one set of grandparents' houses or the other, with tables laden with food and rooms filled with laughter, created a rhythm that we all cherished.

I remember those paternal Sundays best. Five or six of us cousins would crowd around the wood-fired stove in my grandparents' kitchen, our eyes fixed on Nanna as she made her famous meatballs. We would hover, trying to sneak bites before she noticed, playing the same game every week. It was a ritual that had no need for words; it was a dance we all knew by heart.

These weren't just traditions; they were part of who we were. They were our inheritance, a bond forged in love, laughter, and shared history.

We didn't need to be told who we were. We experienced it. We could taste it in the food that was served, hear it in the cadence of our parents' voices, and see it in the way they cared for one another, even when their opinions didn't always align.

They worked hard, loved even harder, and clung to the values passed down from across the ocean and through Ellis Island. Their generation didn't just reap the benefits of their parents' sacrifices. They honored them. Each meal shared, each holiday celebrated, and each act of generosity or discipline added another brick to the foundation that began with nothing more than twelve dollars and a third-class ticket.

Interlude: The Day the Ground Shook

On September 12, 1940, the ground in Morris County trembled. Not from a storm or an earthquake, but from the most catastrophic industrial disaster the region had ever known.

At 1:30 in the afternoon, close to 300,000 pounds of gunpowder detonated at the Hercules Powder Factory in Kenvil, New Jersey. The explosion was so powerful it was felt as far away as New York City, fifty miles from the site. Windows shattered for miles. Cars jolted off the roads. Telephone wires collapsed. Merchandise flew off store shelves. And inside Dover High School, terrified students screamed and fled their classrooms, some instinctively knowing that their world had just changed.

Fifty-one workers were killed that day.

Among them was my uncle, Ralph Granato, my mother's brother.

What makes this loss particularly piercing is that three men in our family were on the payroll at that factory. They were all scheduled to work that day, three relatives, one shift, one catastrophic moment, but only two came home.

My grandfather had the day off, a rare and well-earned pause from a life of endless labor. My father, in an unexpected decision that would never be questioned again, stayed home sick. But Ralph, still young, just beginning to build a life of his own, reported for duty. He did what so many men in our family had always done. He clocked in, worked without complaint, and assumed he would clock out at the end of the day. He never got the chance.

There is a silence that follows a tragedy of that kind. Not the absence of noise but a heavy stillness that lingers longer than the blast itself.

No one in our family could make sense of it. My mother carried that day in her heart for the rest of her life. So did my father. It wasn't only the loss, the harrowing images, or the chaos that overtook Dover General Hospital, where bodies were placed on the lawn because there was no space inside. It was the nearness of it. The randomness. The haunting knowledge that it could have been any of them. It nearly was.

In time, the plant was rebuilt, production resumed, and life pressed on. And so did our family, forever marked but never broken.

We carry stories like that in our blood. Stories that never quite make the history books but shape the way we see the world. The way we value a single day, a single breath, a single twist of fate.

For me, the 1940 Hercules explosion is more than a footnote in local history. It's a line carved into the stone of my family. It's the day that took one of ours, and spared two others. It's a reminder that every ordinary day is a miracle waiting to be seen.

Reflection

My parents were each raised in homes where survival often came at the expense of tenderness. Love wasn't always spoken, and security was a fleeting hope rather than a guarantee. My grandparents did what they could with what little they had. They were fierce, resourceful, and unyielding in their determination. But beneath that exterior of strength lay profound pain, a pain that was often left unspoken, with stories that were never fully shared.

My father, in particular, carried a deep sense of not belonging. It was a wound he never fully explained but which often expressed itself through control, anger, and an overwhelming need to prove his worth to the world. My mother, quieter and more reserved, carried her heavy burdens, a history of betrayal and loss. Together, they were two people who had been raised in the chaos of their pasts, each trying to build something stable out of the broken pieces they had been given. It wasn't always perfect, sometimes far from it, but it was real.

As I grew older, I began to see my parents as more than just "Mom and Dad." I began to see them as people broken and brave, shaped by the ghosts of their pasts. And it was through this understanding that forgiveness finally took root.

Ralph Granato – Gone too soon, your spirit remains untamed

Chapter Five

The Fabric of Family Unfiltered & Unbreakable

"Celebrating the Messy & Marvelous Journey"

In our family, therapy wasn't a sterile office with a stranger scribbling note; it was a dining table surrounded by nine uncles and six aunts, each offering advice with a side of pasta. Our therapy sessions were loud, messy, and full of heart. Heated debates, raucous laughter, and stories told with unapologetic honesty were the cornerstones of our discussions.

We didn't do small talk. Conversations flowed in full volume, unfiltered, with hand gestures that could knock over a glass of wine. We argued passionately, laughed freely, and forgave before the last spoonful of sauce was scraped from the pot.

There was an unspoken rhythm to the chaos, a kind of sacred dance that held us together. Our love was loud, unapologetic, and all-encompassing. No one ever left our family gatherings hungry or without feeling challenged.

We were a family that lived life in bold strokes, painting our story with vibrant colors that refused to be muted. Our fabric was a tapestry of mismatched personalities and intertwined histories, each thread contributing to a pattern that was uniquely ours.

It wasn't always neat, orderly, or quiet. But it was ours a messy, chaotic, beautiful masterpiece. We were the Basenese family, and our story was one of laughter, love, and the kind of madness that only a family could truly understand.

A Family Tapestry
"The Vibrant Characters That Wove Our Story"

We weren't just a family; we were a patchwork of vibrant characters, as diverse and colorful as the ingredients in Aunt Anna's famous meatballs. Each person brought their blend of quirks, humor, and unwavering loyalty, coming together to form a tapestry that was uniquely ours: complicated, lively, and undeniably full of life.

There was Uncle Angelo, the self-appointed comedian whose sharp wit could turn any conversation into a comedy routine, often at the expense of some unsuspecting relative. Aunt Anna, in contrast, was our local source of gossip, her stories more riveting than any tabloid, and her meatballs were legendary, rumored to have healing properties that went beyond the kitchen.

Aunt Mary stood as the matriarch, embodying the strength and command of a figure like Don Corleone. Her presence alone demanded respect, and her words weighed with quiet authority. On the other hand, Uncle Patsy and Uncle

Domenick were the silent giants of the family. Their strength and wisdom were often unspoken but deeply felt, offering a steady anchor in the storm of family life.

Every family gathering felt like a reunion of archetypes. Uncle Mike was the teacher-turned-businessman, equally adept at grading papers or closing deals, always ready to take on any challenge. Uncle Anthony was our peacekeeper, his calming influence diffusing tensions with a well-placed word or a knowing smile, bridging divides with grace and quiet understanding.

Uncle "Stacky," Frank, to some, was the steady hand, his stoic demeanor providing a sense of calm amidst the lively chaos. Then there was Falieu, or Raffaello, the family's gentle soul, often overshadowed by louder voices but whose kindness and soft nature left a lasting impact. Finally, there was Uncle Pat, Joseph, as he was formally known as our career Navy man, whose military precision and sense of order lingered even when he sat back at the family table, no longer in uniform but still a pillar of respect.

Together, they formed a harmony that was unmistakably Basenese. Each contributed their unique note to our family symphony one of laughter, loyalty, and a touch of madness that defined who we were.

Birthdays, baptisms, funerals, and sacred Sunday dinners weren't just occasions; they were lifelines. They were the threads that wove us together, holding us in place through time and telling the story of who we were. Through every meal, every toast, and every shared glance, we reaffirmed that unspoken pledge: "We're still here, and we're still us."

Our gatherings were more than meals or holidays. They were a ritual of reconnection, a reaffirmation of the invisible threads that kept us bound, no matter how unraveled life became. In a world that constantly pulled us in different directions, these family traditions served as anchors. They reminded us that even when money was tight, hearts were bruised, or careers fell off course, we had each other. People who would roast you mercilessly one moment and defend you to the grave the next. People who made you laugh until your stomach hurt and drove you up the wall, sometimes all before dessert. Family wasn't just a word. It was our currency, our compass, our safety net... and yes, sometimes, our chaos.

Tempers had their place at the table, too. Love in our family didn't whisper; it shouted, slammed cabinets, and sometimes squared off over sausage, like that infamous Easter when two uncles nearly came to blows over the last link on the platter. It wasn't about the sausage, not really. One hadn't spoken to the other since 1961 over a borrowed wrench that was never returned. The sausage was just the match that lit a fire already smoldering for decades. And yet, just as quickly, it burned out. A few muttered words, a shoulder slap, a shared glass of wine, and a gruff "fuggedaboutit" would settle things. Forgiveness in our family didn't come wrapped in flowery speeches. It came in gestures, in shared meals, and in the unspoken agreement that life was too short to carry a grudge past the cannoli.

Holidays were grand performances of love, food, and familial theatrics. Thanksgiving looked like a casino banquet hall; tables stretched end to end, overflowing with turkey, lasagna, sausage stuffing, candied yams, and enough homemade wine to power a small sailboat. One uncle always passed out in the recliner by halftime, while at least two aunts inevitably got into it over how much salt belonged in the gravy. Kids ran amok, tripping over plastic-covered rugs in pursuit of cookies they were absolutely forbidden to eat before dinner.

And Christmas Eve? That was our masterpiece. The Feast of the Seven Fishes wasn't just a meal. It was a production. Baccalà, calamari, shrimp, mussels, eel, and smelts are sea creatures that terrified us as children but somehow disappeared when battered and fried. Somewhere between the linguine and the espresso, someone would bring up politics, or worse, religion and all hell would break loose. Voices would rise, chairs would screech, and someone would dramatically declare they were leaving.

But no one ever did.

Because in our family, leaving wasn't really an option. The family was non-negotiable. You could argue, cry, sulk, and threaten, but at the end of the night, you stayed. You ate dessert. You passed the espresso. You showed up again next time.

We didn't need television or performers. We were the entertainment. Our gatherings held the rhythm of a living play, part drama, part comedy, part suspense, with at least one aunt delivering a tearful monologue by dessert.

At the heart of it all were the cousins, a chaotic coalition of kids without matching jackets but bound by secret codes and shared adventures. We tore through backyards like outlaws, invented games no adult could follow, and whispered secrets into closet walls as if the truth might unravel us. We were allies one minute and rivals the next. Backup singers. Co-conspirators.

The fabric of our family wasn't stitched from anything delicate or rare. It was denim and burlap tough, frayed, familiar. It bore the marks of time, rubbed soft by years of use and love, worn thin in places but never torn beyond repair. And still, it held. It was held through baptisms and breakups, through hospital vigils and late-night dances in the kitchen. Through laughter that echoed too loudly and silences that said everything. Through fights that stung and forgiveness that came not with fanfare but with a shrug and a plate of leftovers.

Our love was never gentle, but it was unwavering. It wrapped itself around us in the form of unsolicited advice and rib-crushing hugs. It showed up loudly, stubbornly, and messily, but it showed up.

In the end, the Basenese family fabric was held together not by politeness or perfection but by a relentless, sometimes reckless love. We were stitched from the same bold thread: sharp-witted, sharp-tongued, fiercely loyal, and absolutely unforgettable. Our characters were larger-than-life saints in their own eyes, comedians in everyone else's, stubborn as mules, funny as hell, and loyal beyond reason.

Maybe someday, in another book, I'll tell more of their stories, the ones who lit up the room and flipped tables when they didn't get their way. The ones whose quirks became legends, whose names still stir laughter and tears. For now, just know this: I come from people who knew how to show up. Not perfectly. Not quietly. But with presence, with passion, with love.

And that love, gritty, relentless, unshakable, became the ground beneath my feet. It carried me through moments when I couldn't see my strength. It showed up in ways I didn't always recognize until long after the dishes were cleared and the guests had gone home. That fabric, patched and loud and wildly vibrant, became the net beneath every leap I took.

It made me brave.

It made me whole.

And for that, I carry nothing but gratitude.

Chapter Six

Sundays, Sacraments & Sauce

"A Celebration of Family, Faith, and Flavor"

In our house, Sunday wasn't just a day on the calendar. It was the heartbeat of the week. It began in church and ended at the family table, with everything in between drenched in the rituals that defined us. There was Mass, there was marinara, and there were moments so sacred they blurred the line between the holy and the chaotic.

If you didn't grow up Italian American, you might think Sunday was for sleeping in or catching up. But in our world, it was a living, breathing performance of faith and family. The script stayed mostly the same, the cast rarely changed, but each week delivered its unscripted surprises.

We rose early as if summoned. We dressed like we were headed to meet royalty because, in our minds, we were. Heaven was watching. I can still feel the scratch of starched collars and the shine of shoes polished the night before. The air inside the church was thick with incense, curling like whispered prayers through beams of stained-glass light. The pews were filled with wrinkled hands clutching rosaries and old voices belting out Latin hymns slightly off-key but filled with fervor. That was our soundtrack. That was our sanctuary.

Our family's pew was more than a place to sit; it was an altar of memory. God was not some distant force. He was present, personal, and fully engaged, especially when Nanna talked to Him aloud like He was sitting beside her. And if you dared to squirm or whisper, you'd meet a glare from a parent so sharp and silent it could stop your heart mid-beat. No words were needed. You just knew.

But the true act of devotion came after Mass. That's when worship turned tangible. We went home, not to rest, but to cook, to gather, to celebrate in the language our family understood the best food. By the time we opened the front door, the house had already been transformed, not into some quiet, angelic haven but into something altogether holier: a kitchen alive with the scent of garlic, tomatoes, onions, basil, and beef all working in harmony. The air was thick with aroma and memory. You didn't just smell it. You felt it. You walked in and were embraced by it. The sauce didn't simmer. It sang. You could almost hear it calling out, "Mangia… I've been waiting."

Brunch didn't exist in our vocabulary. There was only Sunday dinner, and it wasn't a meal. It was a marathon. We sat down at one, and no one knew when we'd leave. Hours melted away under the spell of red sauce and laughter. The table groaned with offerings: meatballs, sausage, pork neck bones, and braciole, all nestled in a pot so enormous it could've christened a toddler. The pasta wasn't a dish; it was a ceremony. The salad always served afterward, felt like a footnote. And dessert wasn't negotiable, no matter how full you were. You made room for cannoli. You had to. Not partaking would've been borderline sacrilege.

These weren't just meals. They were sacred rituals. The table became our altar, the sauce our sacrament, and the family our congregation. Every Sunday, we didn't just eat together. We bore witness to something ancestral, something bigger than any one person. It was the kind of gathering that bound generations across time and memory.

Everyone had a role to play. The women ran the kitchen as seasoned commanders, aprons tied with purpose, wooden spoons wielded like batons conducting an orchestra. Their voices bounced between sharp commands and gentle blessings, often in the same breath. There was love in their labor, though it wasn't always gentle. It came fast, loud, sometimes biting, but always from the heart. The men, meanwhile, circled the kitchen and table like satellites in orbit, wine in hand, sneaking pieces of bread to dip into the pot when they thought no one was looking. Arguments erupted with ease over baseball scores, crooked politicians, who was the cheapest uncle, or who stole Nanna's last pizzelle. None of it mattered, really. It was the sport of being together.

The children filled every space in the chaos. We ducked under tables, took over the backyard, and turned basements into fortresses. We invented games with rules no adult understood. We forged alliances, settled disputes with stickball, and plotted revolutions that usually ended with someone crying or bleeding. We lived in our universe within the family cosmos, always on edge, waiting for that inevitable call either to eat or to quiet down before we attracted the wrath of a grown-up trying to hear themselves talk.

And yet, for all the movement and noise, there was something steady at the core. There was a structure in the tradition. There was reverence in the repetition. No matter how loud we got, we all understood certain things remained untouched, inviolable.

There was respect. Deep, unwavering, sometimes unspoken, but always enforced. Respect for the grandparents who built the life we were now enjoying. Respect for the elders whose stories were long and winding and, more often than not, repeated. Respect for the food itself, which was never just food. It was history, art, and offering. You didn't turn your nose up at the sauce. You didn't pour your wine unless you were told to. You never corrected someone older, even when their facts were wildly off. These weren't mere rules. They were immutable laws passed down like scripture. And when broken, the punishment wasn't always a slap. Sometimes it was a look. Sometimes, a story pierced you straight through, leaving you so guilt-ridden you wished for a slap instead.

Now and then, amidst the roar of voices and the scraping of plates, a pause would emerge. It might last a moment or only a breath. But in that space, you could feel something press in from the edges. A quiet reminder that this was more than a meal. This was a legacy being written in real-time. This was a ritual older than all of us. In those silences, you understood: the sauce might evolve, the faces would grow older or disappear, but the soul of these Sundays, the union of faith, food, and family, would outlast every one of us.

Before the first fork even grazed the pasta, we prayed. Not a hurried "Bless us, O Lord," said with one eye on the garlic bread, but a genuine moment of stillness. Heads bowed. Hands folded or resting beside plates. Nanna always led. Her voice was low and steady, a voice you didn't talk over. Sometimes, she prayed in English, but more often in Italian, her words thick with a kind of beauty we didn't need to translate. No one reached for a thing until she finished. It wasn't just etiquette. It was a sacred order. A sign that before we fed our bodies, we nourished our spirit.

If someone forgot to cross themselves, they didn't get away with it. A sharp elbow from a relative or a whispered "testa di legno" (blockhead) was all it took to bring the moment back into focus. In our family, God came first, even before the meatballs hit the table.

Sacraments weren't just dates on a church calendar. They were events that mobilized the entire community. First Communions brought white dresses stiff with starch and boys sweating through too-tight suits. Families gathered on church steps, snapping photos in the sun, flashbulbs popping like paparazzi at a movie premiere. What came next was just as sacred: a celebration with enough food to feed a small army. Confirmations were part holy ceremony, part extended family reunion, and part unspoken contest over which godparent gave the most generous envelope.

Even the smallest rituals held significance. Rosary beads hanging from the rearview mirror weren't decoration. They were protection. Kissing the crucifix before leaving the house was as natural as locking the door. Lighting candles for the dead wasn't superstition. It was communion with those who had gone before us. And every once in a while, someone would decide it was time to go to confession. Not because they were in mortal sin but because the soul needed dusting off. A clean slate meant a clear conscience. And in a house where emotions could rise from calm to chaos in less than a minute, peace was a precious and necessary commodity.

Faith wasn't dissected or explained in long conversations. It was soaked into the foundation of everything. It lived in the walls of our home, in the anxious pacing of our grandparents, in the way wine was poured, and in the worry etched into every parent's forehead. Faith was felt more than taught. It came through touch; the holy water traced across your brow before walking out into the world. It came through consistency in the way certain things were always done, without question or complaint.

It taught us how to hold on. No matter how exhausting the week had been, Sunday would bring us back to balance. No matter what fights had flared up between siblings, spouses, or generations, the table always allowed for softening for some version of reconciliation. No matter what storm Monday might bring, we had been restored not only by food but by grace, not just by ritual but by presence, not just by God but by one another.

As a kid, I didn't always understand it. I didn't know how deeply these patterns were forming the framework of my belief. But looking back now, I see it clearly. My faith didn't take root in the homilies or catechism classes. It came from the faces around that table. It came from the steam rising from a bowl of ziti, the scent of garlic in the air. It came from my mother's voice echoing up the stairs, calling me to get ready for Mass. It came from my father's steady presence, rarely speaking but always kneeling. His prayers were silent, but they were loud in their way.

This wasn't religion as a requirement. It was faith as daily breath. It was messy and flawed, soaked in sauce and surrounded by noise. But it was real. It lived in us and around us. It moved with us. And somehow, even in the imperfections, it was holy.

If ever there was a home that embodied the full spectrum of faith, its seriousness, its superstition, and the strange comfort it could offer, it was my maternal grandmother's house in Port Morris. Nanna's home was more than a residence. It was a sacred stage where the holy and the theatrical played out side by side in perfect harmony. A place where belief wore both a halo and a raised eyebrow.

To enter her home was to pass through a kind of spiritual checkpoint. The indoor porch wasn't just a space to remove your shoes. It was a vestibule to the divine. Its high ceiling loomed over an L-shaped shelf that bore a battalion of Catholic saints, each poised in silent anticipation, like celestial soldiers waiting for their next assignment. Beneath them, vigil candles glowed with steady purpose. Their flames were more than fire. They were indicators of divine favor or its withdrawal.

If a candle was unlit, it meant something had gone wrong. A prayer was unanswered, a petition ignored. The saint responsible would be placed in temporary exile, their flame snuffed out as both warning and protest. This wasn't done lightly. It was Nanna's way of holding heaven accountable. No glow, no grace. The candle would remain dark until the saint made good on their part of the deal.

As children, we quickly learned the unspoken ritual. Before even looking at Nanna's face, we'd scan the shelf. Saint Anthony's flame still danced? Good—something had been found. Saint Jude's candle cold and dark? Trouble. Someone upstairs had dropped the ball. And if you asked about it, you'd better be prepared for a story, possibly a monologue, and definitely a glare sharp enough to make glass sweat.

That porch was more than a room. It was a theater of devotion, a stage where belief flickered, flared, or faltered but never disappeared. Faith wasn't fragile there. It was bold. It was personal. It had personality. It could be frustrating, furious, or even a little petty. But it was always active. Always alive.

Looking back now, I understand what I couldn't see then. Faith doesn't have to be serene to be sincere. It doesn't always wear white robes or whisper prayers in hushed tones. Sometimes, it slams doors, extinguishes candles, and demands answers. But it stays. Even when it wrestles with itself, it stays.

Our Sundays were rarely quiet. The saints sometimes faced divine suspension. Our prayers didn't always yield miracles. Still, we showed up. We prayed. We laughed. We argued. We relit candles. We kept the ritual alive. In doing so, we learned something no sermon could teach: belief is not measured by how still its flame burns but by the courage it takes to light it again when it goes out.

Nanna "The matriarch of Port Morris, half-saint,
half-sorceress" with my sister Ruth

The Granato Family – My mother Eva's family

Chapter Seven

Wakes & Weddings

"What We Lost"

"The Joys and Heartaches that Shape Us"

In an Italian family, a funeral and a wedding aren't as different as outsiders might think. Both require formal attire, sacred words, the shedding of tears, disputes over seating arrangements, and a banquet of food that feels too large for the occasion. The difference lies in the opening act. One begins with vows and the other with eulogies, but both are declarations of love, legacy, and loyalty. And in our family, we never missed an opportunity to show up. We arrived in full force, whether for celebration or sorrow, loud and loyal, dressed impeccably, and armed with prayers and stories.

As a child, I often mistook wakes for some kind of sad gathering that teetered on the edge of a party. Rooms filled with relatives in dark, solemn clothing, rosary beads clutched tight in their fingers, their lips moving silently or whispering bits of family news near the casket. The air was dense with the mingled scent of lilies and espresso. Someone would inevitably laugh at the wrong time. It wasn't disrespectful. It was a memory surfacing in the form of humor because, in our world, grief never stood alone. It always came paired with the stories that made us love and lose in the first place.

We told tales at wakes the way other families reserved them for wedding receptions. With overflowing hearts, wine that loosened tongues, and a need to bring the departed back to life for just a little while through the power of recollection. We couldn't bury someone until we resurrected them in stories, in laughter, in the kind of shared remembrance that made absence feel briefly suspended.

The meal after a funeral was never just a meal. It was a ritual. Plates of macaroni cooked with mourning, sausage and peppers served with sorrow. You didn't eat because you were hungry. You ate because chewing, crying, and talking were ways to keep the grief from hollowing you out. It was how we coped together, around a table, forks in hand, hearts cracked open.

Then, just as grief settled into our bones, along came the noisy, lavish weddings, sometimes fraught with family tension but always pulsing with joy. Invitations carried weight. Absences were noted. Gifts were tracked. The politics could be exhausting, but beneath all of it was a quiet thrill: the family was growing, reshaping itself, finding something new to hold on to.

Mourning, in our family, never happened in silence. The aunts mourned like opera singers, each one vying to express the deepest pain. Wails filled the room like arias of agony. Sobs whispered prayers in dialect, clutching rosaries with hands that trembled more from feeling than from age. It was grief performed and lived at full volume, raw and real. If you walked into the wake blindfolded, you might have thought someone had been physically wounded. The sorrow was that palpable.

But even the grief had rhythm. It rose and fell like a gospel chorus, with each voice adding a layer of texture and truth. It was unfiltered. It was deeply sincere. And even when it spilled into a spectacle, no one ever doubted its depth.

When it came to weddings, we brought the same passion we had for funerals, just tuned to a different frequency.

Every Italian wedding came with an unspoken tradition, passed down from generation to generation like a sacred, slightly shameful heirloom: someone always drank too much and grabbed the wrong person's ass. Usually, an uncle. Sometimes, a cousin. Always someone old enough to know better and full of enough Chianti to stop caring. It was inevitable. As the music soared and the drinks flowed, it would happen like some twisted rite of passage, an "accidental" hand placed just a little too low, followed by a slap, a gasp, and a near-brawl by the dessert table.

You could almost hear Sinatra crooning in the background: "I've got the world on a string... and Uncle Joe on probation."

There were shouts and accusations, hands waving, coats being yanked off chairs. But before the cake was ever sliced, it always simmered down. That was how we did things. We might brawl like alley cats, but we forgave like we were born to do it.

And then there was the food.

There was never any need for a miracle to turn water into wine. We were already four bottles deep before the antipasto hit the table. The spread was glorious: platters piled high with cured meats and cheeses, olives, peppers, and artichokes. Lasagna, baked ziti, veal parmigiana, roast beef, and chicken cutlets. Salad that no one touched, bread that never stopped coming. And dessert? Cannoli stuffed to bursting, rainbow cookies in endless colors, a wedding cake the size of a baptismal font, and espresso strong enough to revive the nonni we just buried last fall.

These weren't elegant affairs held in gilded ballrooms with plated dinners and hired quartets. Ours took place in American Legion halls, VFW basements, and Elks Lodge rec rooms venues with low ceilings, sticky floors, loud laughter, and buffet tables longer than some of the marriages they celebrated.

The moment you walked in, you were hit with a blast of accordion music, too much cologne, and the soft haze of cigarette smoke hanging in the air like a fog of memories. The guest list was always sprawling: cousins, cousins-of-cousins, neighbors, in-laws, exes, and even the guy who once helped the groom tile a bathroom and somehow got an invite.

The food arrived in waves, unstoppable and unapologetic. Mountains of pasta, vats of meatballs, bottomless trays of baked ziti that could violate fire codes. And at the bar, the wine flowed with ease, chased by whiskey, anisette, and whatever Grandpa had hidden in his trunk "just in case the bartenders ran dry."

Which, of course, they never did because the family made sure of it.

Another cherished tradition at Italian weddings was keeping an eye on the servers. Not out of paranoia, well, maybe a little, but mostly because everyone knew someone working the event would eventually try to sneak a bottle or a tray of leftovers out the back door.

They never got away with it.

There was always an uncle, a cousin, a godfather-type strategically posted near the kitchen "just to help out," conveniently there the moment some poor 18-year-old waiter tried to tuck a bottle of Chianti under his coat.

"Hey… HEY! Where Are you going' with that, Tony?"

Cue the red cheeks, the stammered apology, and the slow walk of shame back to the bar.

In our family, generosity was expected. Stealing, especially wine, wasn't. The wine wasn't just booze; it was a sacrament.

But for all the fanfare and chaos, it was my father's funeral that stood apart.

Three days of viewing. Every afternoon and evening. The family showed up and stayed. Nobody slipped in late or ducked out early. That wasn't how we did death. You stood. You wept. You held the hand of someone who looked like your father did at your age, and you wondered how time moved so fast.

The Mass was beautiful, but the burial was hard. The meal afterward offered a brief moment of breath as tears fell silently into soup bowls and bread-soaked up grief beside trembling hands.

But what remains etched in me more than anything is the sheer magnitude of presence. His funeral wasn't just a goodbye. It was a procession of respect. I swear, fifteen hundred to two thousand people came to pay their dues. Politicians. Tradespeople. Old neighbors. New friends. People I'd never seen before but who somehow knew him.

It felt like watching a statesman be laid to rest. But he wasn't a senator or a public figure. He was a butcher. A cop. A father. A fixer. A force.

And that's when I understood something that I'd never put into words before:

Legacy isn't written in stone. It's written in footsteps.

Reflection

Looking back, it's almost impossible to separate the wakes from the weddings. Both were ways we marked time, not just dates on a calendar, but declarations of what mattered. They were how we kept people from fading quietly into memory.

At weddings, we celebrate the beginning of something sacred. At funerals, we honor the end of something beloved. In both, we turn to the only tools we have ever truly trusted: food, family, and faith, not always in that order.

We laughed at funerals because grief, for us, came braided with joy. We cried at weddings because we understood how fragile happiness could be.

What I've come to see is that these moments, the big ones, the loud ones, weren't just ceremonies. They were anchors. They held us to our past, grounded us in our people, and reaffirmed an unspoken promise: family shows up.

Even in loss, we gathered. Even in joy, we remembered those who were missing.

And through it all, from the wine-slicked floors of the Elks Lodge to the quiet pews of the funeral parlor, we remained connected. Not perfectly. Not without conflict. But with devotion. With force.

Because that's who we were. That's who we still are.

Chapter Eight

The Day I Died
"And Lived, in Laura's Hands"

"Finding Life in the Hands of Love"

July 6, 2006, a date scorched into my memory, was the day I died. Just twenty days shy of my 57th birthday, death came without warning, without ceremony. One moment, I was walking beside Laura in Newport Beach, California, and the next, I collapsed, a sudden-death heart attack claiming me in an instant.

For twelve long minutes, I was gone.

No pulse.

No breath.

No life.

Clinically dead. Legally gone. Spiritually vacant. Snuffed out.

But this is not where the story ends.

Laura, with nothing but love, instinct, and refusal in her veins, dropped to her knees and began the work of resurrection. One compression at a time, she fought death with bare hands and belief.

She didn't scream. She acted.

She didn't freeze. She moved.

Her hands, steady and desperate, breathed life back into me. With every push against my chest, she defied the finality of death. When the paramedics arrived, they found her still there sweating, locked in focus, unwavering, performing CPR as if she were holding back a tide with her bare body. Because to her, I wasn't a body. I was still worth saving. They took over. The sirens wailed. Machines, wires, and flashing lights swallowed me. And then, somewhere amid the noise, a heartbeat. I lived. But not as the same man.

And then there was Laura.

Laura didn't just bring me back to life that day; she has always been the steady force keeping my heart beating. Through the pressures of life, through loss, heartbreak, success, and everything in between, she has been the unwavering foundation. In a family no stranger to turbulence, Laura has been the rock, the shelter in the storm. She prayed for our children when I was consumed by work, soothed my hardened spirit when it needed softness and remained by my side when life pressed us down with its heavy burdens.

Through every version of myself, the insecure son, the ambitious man, the grieving father, the businessman, and the boy endlessly seeking approval, Laura's love has never wavered. It has been the constant, the guiding light, a reminder of what true devotion looks like, of the unbreakable bond between two souls. In the darkest days, when I emerged changed, broken, and renewed, Laura stood by me, her love unwavering, a beacon that led me back to life and hope.

Laura saved my life that day. Not figuratively, but literally.

According to the doctors, it was her swift and precise CPR that made the difference between life and death for me. If not for those precious minutes and those perfectly executed compressions, I wouldn't be here to share this story. I wouldn't just have been unable to walk or talk. I would have been gone from this world, from everything.

We had just finished a brisk five-mile walk down Newport Coast Drive to the ocean and back. The sun was beginning its descent, casting a warm glow over everything, and the cool Pacific breeze still clung to our skin as we casually discussed dinner plans, something light and simple. I was walking beside her when, without warning, the world went dark.

There was no cry, no stumble, no indication. One moment, I was there alive, engaged, and the next, I was falling. It wasn't a slow collapse but a sudden, jarring loss of control, like a plank of wood knocked from a rooftop. I hit the ground, crashing backward, but by some miracle, I missed the unforgiving concrete sidewalk. Instead, I landed on the slightly more forgiving blacktop, sparing my skull from certain destruction.

Laura's reaction was instinctual. She sprinted toward me, a primal drive overtaking her. She saw the color drain from my face, and, in that moment, she knew. I was dying.

In that moment, Laura became the hero of this story not simply a bystander or loving partner, but the decisive force who refused to let death have the final word. She dropped to the ground beside me, positioning herself between my lifeless body and whatever darkness threatened to take me, her entire being focused on one mission: to keep me here.

My mouth was slack and open, breathless. My eyes were vacant, void of any light. She recognized the signs instantly. My tongue had slipped back and blocked my airway. Without flinching, she reached into my mouth and forced her fingers down my throat. My jaws clamped shut in reflex, nearly crushing her fingers, but she didn't pull back. She kept going, guided by instinct, pain, and the urgent rhythm of love. Her hands worked blindly and relentlessly until the blockage was cleared.

Only then did she begin CPR. It had been over twenty years since she was last trained, but her body remembered what my heart had forgotten. She laced her fingers together, locked her elbows, and started compressions with precision and resolve. Each push into my chest was a plea to the universe and a command to my body. Breathe. Come back. Stay.

As she worked, she let out a piercing whistle, a sharp, slicing sound that carried beyond the quiet condos into the open air. It was not panic. It was purposing a call to action. Within moments, three neighbors emerged and saw what she was fighting against: a man without breath and a woman who refused to let go.

Though unsure and trembling, the neighbors were swept into Laura's orbit. She didn't ask. She led. With a clarity that defied the moment, she turned to them and began assigning tasks.

"You, help me with compressions."

"You, breathe for him when I say."

"You, grab the phone and stay on with dispatch. Tell them exactly what I say."

One neighbor had the only working landline, a portable phone with barely enough range to function outside. And yet, against all odds, that fragile signal held. In that critical moment, it became our lifeline. It was as if grace reached through the static, refusing to let go. Laura guided his words as she continued to perform chest compressions, her mind as sharp as her hands were steady. Under her leadership, chaos gave way to structure. The four of them moved as one body, one will, working in rhythm against time.

When panic threatened to break the others, Laura held them steady. When doubt flickered across their faces, her resolve silenced it. Her knuckles whitened, her breath came in short bursts, but she never let go. Through force of love and refusal to lose me, she kept death at bay, not just for a moment but long enough for life to return.

Twelve minutes passed. Twelve minutes without breath, without a heartbeat, without any signal of life. In those long, suspended moments between death and possibility, every second felt like a universe folding in on itself.

When the emergency crew arrived, six paramedics, two medics, and a fire captain found a man with no pulse and no electrical activity on the monitor. The screen was silent. Asystole. The odds were as close to zero as they came. Every protocol in their training said it was time to call it.

But the fire captain didn't.

Something in him resisted that final step. Instead of declaring the time of death, he ordered a round of drug therapy. Then another. He called for one defibrillation. No response. Then another. On the second jolt, the screen came to life: a flicker, then a rhythm. A heartbeat. Against every clinical expectation, life had returned.

I was rushed to Hoag Hospital, one of the top cardiac centers in the country. The initial scans told a brutal truth. A 64-slice CT revealed catastrophic damage to my heart. My widow-maker artery was fully blocked a complete 100%

obstruction. The other arteries were nearly as compromised, showing 90%, 60%, and 40% blockages.

Dr. Tom Benvenuti, a third-generation Italian-American cardiologist, tried to place a stent. But the arteries had deteriorated so severely they bent and twisted under his tools like thin reeds in the wind. The procedure couldn't go forward. My only chance now was open-heart bypass surgery.

Yet even as my heart teetered between repair and collapse, another battle was unfolding. The team of attending physicians wanted to try an experimental treatment-induced hypothermia, a last-ditch attempt to preserve brain function by cooling the body and slowing cellular decay. But standing in their way was the hospital's CEO, who argued for a morphine drip to allow me a quiet, peaceful passing. The procedure had been tried five times before. All five had failed.

But something greater than medicine or policy moved into that hospital that day. The doctors pushed back. They won. And in doing so, they gave me a chance to return.

I was placed in a medically induced coma. The cooling began. The machines hummed. The room watched and waited

When I finally truly came back, I remembered nothing of the fall, the CPR, the twelve minutes without breath, or the coma. But I remember what I saw when I opened my eyes:

Laura, my son, and my sisters gathered around me, their faces washed in disbelief and joy as though witnessing someone rise from the grave.

As they began to recount what had happened, I felt a weight settle into my chest, not a burden, but a purpose. A knowing. Since becoming a born-again Christian in 1991, my faith has shaped how I live, how I give, and how I care for those around me. I've always believed that the Gospel is something to be lived, not just quoted. But from that day forward, I have lived with an unshakable truth, not simply that God is real, but that He saved me.

Through Laura's relentless love, the steady hands of those who refused to give up on me, and the quiet but unmistakable guidance of God, I was brought back from the edge of death. His presence wasn't declared from the heavens. It was felt in the fire captain's refusal to quit, in the medics' urgency, and in the strength that rose in my wife when she needed it most. It was in the moments that defied logic and outlasted reason. It was there all along, steady and unseen.

The story of that day spread far beyond our circle. The Discovery Channel took notice and decided to feature the incident in an episode of their program Call 911. They created a dramatic reenactment of what happened, using actors to bring the event to life. But this wasn't just fiction. It was woven together with real voices. The episode included interviews with those who were actually there: Laura, the fire captain, the dispatcher, the medics, the neighbors who responded, and me. Their words became part of a living record, and the episode reached thousands, maybe millions, sharing a story that began in crisis but ended in triumph.

In the final scene of the broadcast, I said something that still holds weight in my heart: "When we get caught up in things we think are important, like careers or making money, they're not really important. They're just background noise to the real issues in life, which are relationships. You just don't know how much time you have."

I spoke those words because I had lived the truth of them. I had left this world, if only for twelve minutes, and returned with a clarity I had never known before. July 6, 2006, is the day I died and lived again. That date will never leave me. It is a marker in my soul, a testament to what love can do, to what faith can hold, and to what the human spirit can overcome.

My life rested in Laura's hands, literally and figuratively. Her determination, her refusal to accept death, and her love that pushed beyond fear became the bridge between what was and what still could be. I owe my breath, my heartbeat, my every day since then to her.

As I reflect on everything that has followed every meal shared, every handheld, every prayer whispered, I've come to understand something simple and profound. We spend too much time chasing distractions, mistaking them for meaning. But life is in the relationships we nurture, the moments we protect, and the people we choose to love fiercely and without condition.

So, let us hold those we love a little closer. Let us not wait for tragedy to remind us of what matters most. Because even in our darkest moments, when the night is long, and the light is dim, love and faith remain the twin beacons that can guide us home.

Link to Call 911 episode: https://t.ly/lSY-H/call911

QR Code to Call 911 episode

Laura – The angel God sent me from Heaven above

Lou & Laura — A lifetime of grit, grace, and love

Chapter Nine

Becoming a Man, Becoming a Leader

Rising to the Challenge
"A Journey of Growth and Leadership"

The journey toward leadership doesn't begin in boardrooms or with business cards. It starts quietly, often in unlikely places. For me, it began on the cold sidewalks of Netcong, where I learned to walk tall even when the weight of uncertainty pressed down on me. There, I first understood that becoming a man, let alone a leader, wasn't a single defining moment but a steady shaping of the soul forged in discipline, humility, and faith.

Two lessons from my upbringing followed me into adulthood like a constant compass: the burden of my father's expectations and the light of my mother's unshakeable faith. My father's relentless work ethic became my standard; his high standards, though often difficult to meet, taught me how to push myself past comfort and complacency. My mother's kindness reminded me that strength does not have to be loud and that grace often carries more weight than force. Between them, I was taught to lead with integrity, balance grit with heart, and ambition with compassion.

Nothing I achieved came from privilege. There were no shortcuts, no windfalls waiting. What I carried with me was a will that refused to bend, the loyalty of a tightly knit Italian family, and a need to prove not just to my father but to myself and the world that I belonged at the table, that I could build something lasting.

Over the years, I've had the honor of leading divisions within Fortune 500 companies, developing brands from scratch, and negotiating with some of the most formidable minds in private equity. These experiences brought accolades and financial success, but they were never the true measure of my progress. What mattered most was the impact I had on the people around me: Did I create value that went beyond numbers? Did I leave those I worked with better than I found them? Was I building something worth passing on?

My earliest business lessons didn't come from textbooks or lectures. They came from the butcher shop where my father worked, his hands moving with precision and purpose as he prepared each cut. They came from Sundays at my grandmother's table, where uncles spoke in quiet tones about loyalty, risk, and the importance of keeping your word. These moments were my education, unconventional but deeply instructive. They taught me that leadership begins with showing up for others, even when it costs you.

I've never quite fit the polished mold of a CEO. My path didn't follow a linear progression or rely on a traditional pedigree. It was built through persistence, hard work, and a willingness to follow. I learned by doing by making mistakes, taking risks, and owning every misstep along the way.

This path led me through the structured worlds of global corporations and into the raw, unpredictable chaos of startups. I often found myself as the steady hand in unstable environments, helping others navigate risk and rebuild trust. With a mixture of strategy, sweat, and a deep belief in collaborative effort, I helped turn fledgling ventures into thriving businesses.

But the true work was always internal, learning how to lead not just through authority but through presence, empathy, and example. Becoming a man wasn't about achieving status. It was about becoming someone others could count on, someone who didn't flinch under pressure and who never forgot the people who helped him rise.

That's the kind of leader I strive to be. And that's the legacy I hope to leave behind.

Throughout my career, I've been fortunate to lead teams in various industries, from global chemical companies to family-run businesses and consumer product startups. My focus has always been on strategic direction, intentional leadership, and sustainable results. Whether guiding divisions, growing market share, or launching a company from scratch, I have aimed to build trust, redefine norms, and create something lasting.

As a consultant, I've had the opportunity to work with CEOs, decision-makers, and investors, navigating complex transactions with high stakes and expectations. I'm proud of my ability to deliver by facing challenges head-on, making bold decisions, and achieving outcomes that matter.

By shifting the focus away from specific numbers and boasting, this version highlights the key achievements and principles without being overly self-aggrandizing

As my career unfolded, I eventually found myself guiding other companies through turning points, mergers, acquisitions, and high-stakes decisions where trust mattered more than titles. I never saw myself as the smartest person in the room, but I did know how to listen, how to lead when things got uncertain, and how to deliver when it mattered. My edge didn't come from credentials. It came from character and from lessons I first learned in a small town where your handshake meant something and your word meant everything.

Through all of it, I never lost sight of where I came from. The scent of Sunday meatballs bubbling on the stove... the view of the lake from my grandfather's porch at dusk... my father's quiet standards and my mother's fierce devotion, those things stayed with me. They weren't just memories. They were anchors. Reminders that success isn't measured in numbers but in how you carry yourself, how you treat people, and what you leave behind.

Every business I've helped shape, every challenge I've tackled, has required vision. But vision alone doesn't build anything that lasts. That takes grit, the kind forged through hardship, prayer, and holding the line when it would be easier to walk away. It takes loyalty to the people beside you, and the humility to know you can't do it alone.

For me, that steady hand has always been Laura.

The idea for On-Site Fleet Services of Florida started as a whisper, an observation that something was missing in the heavy-duty repair industry. Not just faster service or better tools, but something deeper: a model grounded in trust, built on care. I helped cast the vision, but it was Laura and her brother who brought it to life. They were the ones in the trenches, shoulder to shoulder, before the business had its footing. They were the heartbeat before there was a brand.

And Laura... she was the glue. She faced the long days and hard calls with a quiet ferocity I've always admired. When her brother stepped away after those first few years, it wasn't about filling his place, it was about stepping beside her, where I belonged, as her partner in life and now in business.

By then, the story of On-Site was already being written in her hands. I was simply arriving in time to help turn the page. Together, we built something real, something that grew not just in revenue but in soul. We created a company where people stay because they're seen, because they're valued, because they matter.

We never set out to chase headlines. We chose to pay above-market wages not to make a point, but because it felt right. We built a culture around care, knowing that loyalty is earned, not expected. Today, On-Site is a team of 25, but more than that, it's a family. And Laura? She is still the pulse. Her name is on the ownership documents, yes, but more than that, it's etched into the spirit of the company itself. Her grit, her grace, her goodness... they built the scaffolding. They hold the whole thing up.

This company may have begun as a vision, but it was raised by love. Laura's love for our people, for excellence, for doing things the right way, even when it's hard, that's why it stands strong. And that's why it will outlast us.

The truth is, the values that guide us weren't born in boardrooms. They were born around our kitchen tables. Taught by people who never held business cards but knew how to hold a family together. People who showed up, stayed steady, and prayed us through. That's the legacy we carry forward. And that's the kind of story I'm proud to tell.

My father showed me what it meant to sacrifice. He worked three jobs, not for recognition or accolades, but to ensure that we never felt the sting of lack. He carried the burden silently, never asking for praise, only hoping that his efforts would provide us with something better. My mother, steadfast and faith-filled, offered us the stability we needed. Her calm spirit and trust in something greater grounded us during the most uncertain times. From them, I learned the value of loyalty and the profound importance of treating others with dignity, no matter their role or circumstance.

This wasn't just a company. It was a calling. A dream raised with devotion. And in the end, the real measure of our work won't be found in spreadsheets or financial reports. It will be found in the way we made people feel in the trust we built, the culture we created, and the lives we touched.

These lessons, passed down without pretense, became the blueprint for what we built. It's not merely a business venture; it's a mirror of the values I was raised with. We follow through on our promises. We choose the harder right over the easier wrong, even when it costs more time or effort. And we never forget that behind every invoice, every transaction, every uniform, there is a person with a story that matters

Our culture is one of sincere care. We don't just acknowledge people, we respect them. We support them. We make space for their humanity. Our success is measured not only in outcomes but in the relationships, we foster and the environment we've cultivated. That spirit has made this work more than a job. It's made it a living legacy. A reflection of the home where I first learned that real leadership begins not with a title, but with compassion, consistency, and a commitment to something greater than oneself.

True leadership, as I've come to understand it, is not about accumulating wins or scaling businesses. It goes beyond performance metrics and boardroom outcomes.

Leadership is about being someone others can trust, someone they can rely on in moments of uncertainty.

It means knowing when to lead from the front and when to step back, allowing others to rise in their strengths. It's about listening more than speaking, serving more than commanding, and standing firm in adversity, especially when retreat might seem easier.

Throughout my career, I've had the privilege of leading, building, and creating. But the most profound lessons in leadership didn't come from titles or accomplishments. They came from those who came before me, people who worked with their hands, gave without seeking praise, and built enduring legacies through quiet resilience and sacrifice

As the years have passed, I've come to understand something deeper: success alone cannot satisfy the soul. Sooner or later, something more begins to call. A voice of purpose, of grace, of faith.

And it was only when I slowed down enough to truly listen that faith finally found me.

Chapter Ten

The Faith That Found Me

"An Unexpected Awakening: A Journey to Belief"

On December 2, 1991, I stood barefoot in the soft sand behind the Hilton in Honolulu, Hawaii, attending a beachside church service held during a trade convention. As the waves whispered behind the preacher, I made a decision that would forever change my life: I accepted Jesus Christ as my Lord and Savior. It wasn't a moment born out of spectacle but one of quiet certainty, the realization of a presence that had been gently pursuing me for years. That presence, now unmistakable, was the Holy Spirit.

The man who invited me to that service wasn't a pastor or evangelist. He was a salesman who worked for me, someone who, like many before him, simply refused to give up on me. I had kept my heart guarded, even resistant, but he became the unlikely messenger who helped open a door I had tried hard to keep closed.

My path to Christ was not swift, nor was it easy. I was skeptical by nature, driven by logic and proof. At one point, I even struck a deal with two of my employees at BASF: I would read the Bible from cover to cover, not to seek truth but to discredit theirs. We agreed to meet every weekday morning from 6:30 to 7:00 a.m. I committed to reading twenty pages each night, coming prepared with questions, contradictions, and arguments meant to dismantle their faith. If I succeeded, they would stop speaking to me about God.

But I didn't win that debate.

Somewhere in the Book of Exodus, something shifted. I stopped reading with the intention of disproving. I set aside the red pen of critique and began absorbing the words not intellectually but personally. The text began speaking to me in a way I couldn't explain. I found myself bringing reflections to those morning meetings that even surprised my colleagues. When they asked where my insights were coming from, I didn't have an answer. Now I know: the Holy Spirit had already begun its work in me, reshaping my heart from the inside out.

Long before that pivotal turning point, Laura had been praying for me. She had been a believer well before our marriage in 1988. Her faith was quiet but unwavering, anchored by the steady influence of her father, who passed away at age 59 and her mother, a woman whose strength resided not in persuasion but in presence. The Christmas before my journey began, Laura's mother gave me a Bible. I didn't open it right away, but when I finally did, I realized it wasn't just a gift. It was a seed. A small act that would, in time, grow into something much greater than I could have anticipated.

In 2001, I took a leap of faith and launched my own consulting business, aiming to build and grow consumer brands. I poured in everything I had my time, energy, and belief. But despite months of relentless effort and 18-to-20-hour workdays, the business failed to gain traction. By 2003, the dream had unraveled. Financial pressure mounted rapidly, and the strain began to seep into every corner of our lives, especially our marriage.

Laura, unwavering in her commitment, took a job selling security systems. The income was modest, but it came with good health insurance and gave us just enough to get by. Even so, my response to this season of hardship was far from graceful. I sank into bitterness, unable to separate my identity from the failure that haunted me. Shame clouded my judgment. I withdrew, angry at myself, at life, and even at God.

Eventually, Laura could no longer bear the weight of our fractured relationship. Despite my pleas, she left. Her absence left me shattered. In that hollow space, stripped of excuses and distractions, I found myself reaching out to the only presence that had never turned away: Jesus.

I sought Him with everything I had left. I prayed not for quick fixes but for peace, understanding, and the strength to be remade. After a month of soul-searching and surrender, Laura began her journey back toward our marriage. We were both wounded, but we agreed on one thing: if we were going to rebuild, it would be on the foundation of faith.

By 2004, our financial footing had started to stabilize. But repairing a relationship isn't bound to a balance sheet. The work of restoration was still ahead of us, quiet, continuous, and deliberate.

In July 2006, sensing that we needed time and space to reconnect, we took a six-week trip to Newport Beach, California. It was more than just a vacation. This place had once been a sanctuary for us, a setting where we had grown spiritually and found rhythm in our relationship. We hoped it would offer healing once again.

But only four days into our trip, I suffered what doctors called a "sudden death" cardiac episode. My heart stopped. In those critical moments, my life nearly ended. Yet, by the grace of God, I was brought back.

Later, Laura would say, "It was the best marriage counseling we could have ever received."

The miracle extended far beyond my physical recovery. It reached deep into our marriage and breathed new life into us as a couple. In the aftermath of that brush with death, we were given a fresh start, not just with each other but with the way we lived and loved.

The faith that had found me years earlier on a beach in Honolulu never let go. It had held me through ambition, collapse, shame, and even the edge of death. And it was that same faith, unshaken and steady, that continued to carry us forward.

Reflection

Looking back, I've come to understand that faith isn't something we master or control. It meets us exactly where we are, especially in the moments when we can no longer stand on our own. For much of my life, I leaned on ambition, determination, and intellect to shape my path. But it wasn't until those supports crumbled that I uncovered the foundation that had been quietly holding me all along: Jesus.

He allowed me to break not as punishment but as an opening for renewal. In bringing me to my knees, He taught me the meaning of humility. And through that humility, I began to grow in ways I never could have through strength alone.

Through salvation, pain, and recovery, both spiritual and physical, God revealed something deeper than success or survival. He revealed what it means to be whole.

A Few Brothers Along the Way

Some friendships drift in and out of our lives like the changing seasons. Others remain steadfast through the moves, the marriages, the miles, and the messes. These are the rare bonds that shape who we become. They're the friends who laugh at your worst jokes, stand with you when everything falls apart, and slowly, without asking, become part of your family.

What follows is a tribute to just a few of the men who have walked beside me through the absurd, the sacred, and everything in between my brothers, not by blood but by choice and time.

Mike Leavy - A High School Tale
"Best Friends who Shared Everything"

Lou & Mike — Our Best Years

Some friendships drift in and out of your life like passing seasons. Others show up uninvited, settle in like an old sofa, and stick around surviving everything, even the things no one dares to say aloud. Mike Leavy, my best friend in high school and long after, was one of those rare kinds.

Mike had a charm that could sell snow in January and a mischievous grin that made trouble look like an adventure. He was what you'd get if James Dean grew up in Jersey with a smirk, a rebel streak, and a pocket full of bad ideas. We were inseparable teammates, pranksters, and co-conspirators. Somewhere along the way, we also discovered we had a shared weakness for the same kind of woman. That made things… complicated.

Back in high school, I had an on-again, off-again girlfriend. Our relationship was more of a roller coaster than a romance. I wasn't exactly faithful. I had a habit of chasing whatever

121

sparkled next, even when I already had someone at my side. It wasn't my proudest trait.

Years later, during one of our Netcong Homecoming reunions, Mike pulled me aside. He looked nervous more than I'd ever seen him. At first, I thought maybe he'd eaten something that didn't sit right. But as he started talking, stammering and shifting his weight, I realized it was something heavier.

Finally, after a long pause and a deep breath, he said it. He'd slept with my high school girlfriend after graduation, but still during a time when things between her and me were... unresolved. He wasn't flippant. He looked genuinely ashamed. He wanted forgiveness not just as a friend but as a brother.

I stood there for a moment, letting his words hang in the air. Then I looked him dead in the eye and said, without flinching:

"I know. That's why I slept with your on-and-off girlfriend after I found out."

He went pale. For half a second, I thought I had broken him. And then we both cracked wide, belly-deep laughter that echoed louder than any grudge. The kind of laugh that forgives everything without needing to say the words.

Because that's who we were. Mike and I had shared everything: secrets, screwups, heartbreaks... and, apparently, girlfriends. But what we never lost was the kind of friendship that could take a direct hit and come back stronger. The kind that absorbed blows told the truth and always ended with a bear hug and a joke.

We were boys who grew into men, and somehow, all the chaos just tightened the bond. What we built wasn't fragile. It was forged in experience, sealed with grace, and carried by laughter. And if nothing else, we always had a hell of a story to tell.

The Unbreakable Bond of Paulie and Me
"A Tale of Two Cousins"

Lou & Paulie

Paulie, my cousin and Aunt Anna's beloved son, was just a year older than me. From the start, our lives were bound together two boys growing up under the same roof of family tradition, shaped by the same laughter, chaos, and Sunday dinners. We forged our bond over towering plates of meatballs, hand-me-down wisdom, and the kind of noise only an Italian family gathering can produce.

As the years unfolded, we transformed from wide-eyed kids into mischievous companions and co-conspirators in the beautiful madness of our upbringing. Paulie wasn't just my cousin; he was my closest ally, the brother I never had. We

123

didn't need to explain ourselves to each other. One glance, one smirk, and we knew exactly what the other was thinking. In the unspoken language of family, Paulie spoke fluently.

Uncle Angelo, equal parts charm and chaos, took a special interest in Paulie. He saw something in him, and Paulie rose to meet it. He inherited Angelo's effortless charisma but tempered it with restraint. He was confident, magnetic, and undeniably handsome. When he entered a room, people noticed. I knew I'd never be the main attraction with Paulie around, but being near him was enough. He drew a crowd, and I was glad to be in it.

His voice boomed with the kind of force that commanded a room—rich, unapologetic, and impossible to ignore. Every word was wrapped in a magnetic cadence, sharp as thunder yet smooth as velvet. It didn't ask for attention—it seized it—drawing you in with a strange mix of power and charm, like a storm you couldn't help but watch. There was rhythm in his roar, and in that rhythm, something spellbinding: a presence that made silence feel like a lesser option.

Time moved us into adulthood, and the bond that began in childhood matured. It grew quieter but stronger. Paulie became a man rooted in loyalty and guided by principle. With three sons, a devoted wife, and a work ethic sewn into the fabric of our bloodline, he stood as a living testament to the values our family held dear. He didn't preach those values. He lived them.

Life pulls us in different directions, as it tends to do. But distance meant little. Paulie wasn't the kind of friend who needed checking in every week. He was always there, always steady. Our connection didn't demand attention to survive; it simply was strong, silent, and unshakeable.

When Paulie passed, something in the world shifted. The silence he left behind still echoes. I miss his voice, his laugh, and the ease with which he carried the weight of family. He was a pillar of our story, a thread in the tapestry that held us together. His absence is deeply felt, yet his presence endures in our stories, our memories, and the way we try to love as fiercely as he did.

Paulie was more than a cousin. He was part of the soul of our family, woven into the vibrant, wild, beautiful legacy we inherited and hope to pass on. Though he no longer walks among us, he lives in the echo of our shared laughter, in the strength he gave us by example, and in the love that refuses to fade with time. His story lives on in all of us.

Lou and Frankie

Frankie - "The Soul of Netcong Runs Deep"

If Frankie taught me anything, it's that family isn't always about bloodlines or addresses. It's about loyalty, resilience, and the kind of love that doesn't need to be spoken aloud to be understood. Frankie wasn't just my cousin; he was, and still is, a living reminder of what it means to carry the weight of a legacy and keep walking.

He was born to Uncle "Stacky," Frank, a man built like the machines he commanded. Stacky owned an excavation company with the kind of discipline and force that demanded respect. He worked hard, never asked for credit, and didn't flinch in the face of pain. He was the embodiment of grit. When we lost him in a job-site accident, it sent a shock through our family like someone had ripped out a load-bearing beam from the house we all leaned on.

Frankie bore his father's likeness, not just in appearance but in temperament. He had that same unshakeable calm, the same strength that didn't need to announce itself. Even though he grew up outside of Netcong, his roots were firmly planted there. Every Sunday, without exception, Frankie showed up for Cena at Nanna's. That simple act said everything. Netcong ran through his veins the way love and duty did in our family, unassuming but unbreakable.

In high school, Frankie became a star on the football field at Dover. We couldn't help but beam when his name came up, bragging like he was our quarterback, even when we were miles away from the bleachers. In our eyes, he wasn't just playing the game. He was carrying our town on his back.

During our college years, Frankie and I spent two summers working for Stacky's company. We were more than laborers. We were being shaped. Digging trenches and hauling stones, we learned how to endure and stay steady when the ground beneath us shifted. Stacky didn't just give us a summer job. He gave us a set of values that would stick long after the sunburns faded.

Today, time has done what it does. It moved us forward, gave us families, added gray to our hair and stories to our names. Frankie is a devoted husband, proud father to three daughters and now a grandfather, steady, present, still carrying that quiet strength. When we talk now, it's as if no time has passed. The laughter still comes easy. The memories are still fresh, like the scent of Nanna's sauce lingering in the hallway long after Sunday dinner.

To me, Frankie will always be that same steady presence, the kid who walked beside me through youth and into manhood, the man who never forgot where we came from. He is a piece of Netcong's soul walking around in work boots and humility.

Home, I've learned, isn't just where you live. It's the place that raised you and the people who remind you who you are. It's Sunday supper, the smell of meatballs in the air, the worn hands of our uncles, and the steel in our spines. It's the unshakable bond of blood, yes, but also of shared grit, hard-earned wisdom, and a love that never had to be earned because it was always there.

Frankie, in all his quiet dignity, is proof of that kind of home.

Maxie – "Slapsie Maxie"
The Disco Suit Interview

Max & Colleen

Some people walk into a room, and the atmosphere shifts. Maxie was one of those people. His charisma wasn't loud or forced. It was electric, genuine, and lit from within. With a grin that drew people in and laughter that lifted the air, Maxie had a way of reminding everyone around him that joy was not only possible, but it was also expected. He taught us that personal growth doesn't always unfold in a straight line. Sometimes, it shows up wearing platform shoes, a cream-white leisure suit, and a chest full of confidence.

The name "Slapsie Maxie" wasn't just a nickname. It was an inheritance. Maxie's father, Uncle Mike, earned that title years earlier, hustling grown men on the pool table at Nanna's Hall while standing on stacked soda crates to reach the felt. One night, after wiping the floor with a few unsuspecting challengers, someone in the crowd likened him to the boxer "Slapsie Maxie" Rosenbloom, who had famously danced and jabbed his way through fifteen rounds to victory. The name stuck to Uncle Mike. Years later, it passed to Maxie, dropping the prefix "Slapsie," as though it had waited patiently for the right heir.

Maxie and I first bonded, like so many in our family did, at Nanna's legendary Sunday suppers. I was four years his senior, so at first, I filled the role of mentor, but that didn't last long. What began as guidance quickly grew into camaraderie and then bloomed into brotherhood. Ours was a connection aged over years of shared meals, family chaos, and a love that needed no explanation. It was like vintage Chianti: earthy, lasting, and rich with character.

There's one story about Maxie that perfectly captures his spirit. He had just finished college and was struggling to land a job. One day, he called to say he had an interview near my office. We made plans to meet at Club 80 afterward, a spot where I often unwound with coworkers. When he walked in, time paused. Maxie entered like he owned the place: platform shoes, a cream-white leisure suit, a shirt opened just enough to reveal his famously hairy chest, and a gold chain that caught every glint of light in the room.

I stared at him, stunned.

"You went home to change?" I asked.

He gave me that grin.

"Nope. Came straight from the interview."

I tried to keep a straight face. "How'd it go?"

"Oh, I nailed it," he said, completely unfazed. "Pretty sure they'll make me an offer.'

"How long were you in there?"

"Five, maybe seven minutes."

I paused. "Did anything feel... off?"

"Well," he said, shrugging, "everyone else in the waiting room had on navy suits and ties. A few of them chuckled when I walked in. The receptionist kinda rolled her eyes."

We broke into laughter so hard and deep it pulled something loose inside, something you don't realize you're holding until it's released. That was Maxie. A man who wore his heart, his humor, and his entire outfit on his sleeve.

But Maxie's story isn't just about style or swagger. It's about transformation, the kind that doesn't happen all at once but through steady acts of self-belief. Over time, Maxie reshaped his life. He didn't just change his wardrobe. He redefined his body, rebuilt his confidence, and emerged not as someone reinvented but as someone revealed.

Today, Maxie is a loving husband, a steady brother, a devoted friend, and a source of pride for everyone lucky enough to know him. He shed more than just weight. He let go of old doubts and stepped into his full measure without apology or pretense.

He may have been born Michael, but to us, he is forever Maxie, the one who taught us that reinvention doesn't need permission, that style is sometimes the spark that ignites substance, and that growth, when done right, looks a lot like joy.

In the great family symphony, his laugh still rings through like a favorite melody, timeless, bold, and full of life.

The Cousins   Brotherhood and Laughter

Paulie, A devoted father, with his three sons
Anthony, Vincent & Vito

Chapter Eleven

Losing Christopher

"The Poison That Stole Christopher"

Christopher Neal Basenese

There are moments in life when, we pray, we'll never face chapters we wish didn't have to be written. This is one of them. It is a chapter shaped by pain, grief, and the haunting truth of losing a child far too soon.

My son Christopher was just 37 years old when he died of fentanyl poisoning. It wasn't an overdose in the traditional sense. It was something quieter, more insidious, a counterfeit pill laced with poison that stole him away in an instant. In one breath, my world shattered, and I was forced to live the nightmare that every parent fears.

But his death would be unjust. This story starts with who Christopher was, the life he lived, the people he touched, and the laughter he brought with him everywhere he went.

He was a beautiful soul, radiant with humor, warmth, and the kind of charm that could draw anyone in. Handsome, quick-witted, and effortlessly charismatic, Christopher had the uncanny ability to make you feel like the center of the universe, even in passing conversation. He didn't just enter a room; he lit it up.

We called him "Kramer," after the Seinfeld character, because of his wild entrances, eccentric humor, and endearing unpredictability. I'll never forget when he showed up to his senior prom in a tuxedo with a blow-up doll as his date. That was Christopher bold, irreverent, impossible not to love.

But behind the humor lived a deeper struggle, a silent war he carried in private. Christopher battled addiction for years, caught in a cycle of heroin and Valium. We later learned he was unknowingly self-medicating his undiagnosed bipolar disorder. A counselor once told us that for him, these substances weren't just drugs. They were a way to survive. That understanding shifted everything. It wasn't about weakness or poor choices. It was painful, misread and misunderstood.

Even in the depths of his struggle, Christopher remained a source of strength for others. At his wake, nearly 500 people came to say goodbye. Many were battling their own addictions, some sober, some still fighting, each with a story about how Christopher had helped them. They told us how he'd talked them down from dark places, how he offered comfort when they felt invisible, how he reminded them they mattered.

Those people didn't come only to grieve. They came to testify. To honor the life of someone who, even while struggling, gave so much of himself away.

Christopher's story is not just about loss. It is about the bright, complex, beautiful human he was. He lived with passion, laughed loudly, and loved deeply. And even now, in his absence, his presence continues to be etched into the hearts of all who knew him.

Christopher, my son from a previous marriage, was a constant source of love and pride, a light that shone through even in the most trying times of our family's journey. As his father, I carried an unshakable sense of responsibility to care for and protect him, a devotion that only deepened in the wake of his untimely passing. Laura and I, though not bound by blood to him both, were united in our love for Christopher. In our grief, we stood side by side, determined to honor his memory with dignity, grace, and the reverence he so fully deserved. We found strength in one another and in the memories, we held dear, clinging to them as we navigated the storm of sorrow.

At his service, his brother rose and delivered a eulogy that was as raw as it was beautiful, a tribute not just to a lost sibling but to a bond forged in shared history and unconditional love. Though the room was steeped in grief, the focus remained steadfastly on Christopher's life: his spirit, his laughter, his legacy. Those gathered came not only to mourn but to remember and to offer comfort to one another in the sacred space where grief meets remembrance.

Grief, though, has its language. It can surface in unpredictable forms some loud, some silent. And sometimes, the most powerful response to pain is not to answer it but to let it pass untouched, allowing love to speak in its place. I was given that gift through something far more enduring than any conversation or confrontation: Christopher's own words, written to me from the heart.

Later, at the repast luncheon, I stood to share that letter with those who had gathered. It had been his Christmas gift to me in 2004, a letter of peace, reflection, and healing. It remains one of the most precious things I possess. I carry it with me still, not just in my pocket but in the deepest folds of my soul.

Dear Dad,

I wanted to take this special opportunity to get a few things off my chest. There are a myriad of things I could have given you for Christmas, but there was only one thing I knew you needed.

I want to let you know how much I love you and how grateful I am. With the gestures you have made over your lifetime, especially in the past few months, I have learned the true nature of giving.

I now know where I get my big heart from, and it comes from you. Not many men are as privileged as I am to have such a loving father, and a man who is willing to give his life to his son.

I no longer look into the past, for it only holds contempt. Rather, I gaze into the future, where I see a lifetime of love and happiness, most importantly, a life with you in it.

I know the road may be bumpy at times, but the destination is worth any toll. I look forward to becoming a complete man, and having the missing pieces not only filled in by you, but also crafted by your loving hands.

I want you to save this letter, and whenever doubt may fill our minds, we only have to read this once over to restore the intentions our hearts had all along.

Dad, I want you to know I cherish this opportunity and that I LOVE YOU!

Christopher

After his passing, Christopher left behind a gift, a letter that now lives in my heart like a second heartbeat.

In it, he expressed his love for me and gratitude for the years of unwavering support. He spoke of healing, of the need to look forward rather than back, and of how love and forgiveness have the power to reshape even the most painful pasts. He offered his hopes for a future still unfolding a future marked by growth, reconnection, and the continuation of our journey together, even if now only in spirit.

That letter was his eulogy. Not mine. Not his mother's. It was Christopher, in his own words, telling the world who he was, what he felt, and how he wished to be remembered. No speech could have honored him more fully.

Christopher was a young man I cherished with all my being. I admired his tenacity, fierce humor, and immense heart. Though his battles were great, they never overshadowed the warmth he gave so freely. He had a rare ability to make people feel seen, and even now, his absence is not a void, it's a presence felt in every memory, every quiet moment, every ripple of laughter that echoes unexpectedly.

I think of him every single day. And when I do, I reach for the sound of his laughter, not the silence he left behind. His spirit continues through the stories we share and the love that refuses to leave us.

Grief, I've learned, is not something you get through. It's something you learn to carry. It's not a season that passes but a tide that shifts. It doesn't march forward in a straight line. It spirals, it returns, it transforms.

When you lose a child, grief becomes a constant companion. It never disappears. The waves don't weaken. They simply come less often, giving you time to catch your breath between the storms.

At first, grief feels like a shipwreck. You find yourself submerged in wreckage fragments of memories, familiar scents, and old photographs that float just out of reach. Every breath feels like a betrayal. Every sunrise feels wrong. All you can do is stay afloat, clinging to the love that outlasts even death.

Over time, the waves shift, not in size, but in rhythm. Between them, you find air again. You begin to heal gently, cautiously. But even years later, a song or a scent can bring a wave crashing down. This time, you know you'll survive it. You've been here before. You'll come up, drenched and shaken but breathing.

These wounds, though invisible, are sacred. They're not proof of weakness. They are proof of love, a love vast enough to leave marks. My grief is not a monument to what I've lost; it's a reflection of what I was blessed to have.

I carry Christopher with me in my dreams, my prayers, and the stillness between moments. He was brilliant, stubborn, kind, and imperfect. We both made mistakes, but we always found our way back to each other. His letter is a constant reminder that love endures and that healing is possible.

I miss him every day, but I live, breathe, and love him because he deserves a father who doesn't drift away with the pain but stays, who remembers, and who honors his life by living my own.

I made a promise to him. And I intend to keep it.

*Christopher – A shining light, a
cherished soul – forever in our hearts*

*Chris – bold, brilliant,
and unexpected*

*Chris – living life with
laughter and passion*

"The Last Kiss" — Our final moment, frozen in grace and pain

Chapter Twelve

The Legacy I Carry

"Unbreakable Spirit: The Intersection of Courage, Faith, and Legacy"

I descend from a lineage shaped by hardship and faith, men who carved their lives from ditches and women who lit candles to saints, even when their prayers went unanswered. My beginnings are steeped in the scent of simmering Sunday sauce, the view from wide porches, and the feel of twelve dollars hidden in a coat pocket aboard a steamship. These were symbols of hunger, hope, and the unwavering will to persevere. The roots of my life were formed from faith, grit, loyalty, and a name that bent and reshaped itself seven times before it finally settled.

It was not an entitlement but the sacrifices of those before me that earned me a seat at the table. My father, my mother, my grandparents, and my uncles didn't just raise me. They taught me what it meant to deserve something. They instilled values that could not be unlearned: dignity, presence, and the humility to keep working when no one is watching.

I carry them all with me. I hear Angelo's laughter, remember Louie's resilience, and feel Eva's gentle strength. I can still see Nanna's candles flickering beside her saints, their glow etched into memory, along with the scent of meatballs on the stove and the echo of church bells on quiet streets. I carry a son's voice, now silent, and the enduring strength of a wife who has, more than once, pulled me back from the edge. These echoes, these lives, these lessons in silence, sacrifice, and second chances built the framework of the man I became.

Legacy, to me, isn't just what you inherit. It's what you build brick by brick with every choice, every act of grace, every moment you choose courage over convenience.

I've taken that understanding into every corner of my professional life. I've sat at polished boardroom tables with industry giants and knelt in garages with technicians whose hands reminded me of my uncles. In both settings, I led with the same intention: to build something lasting, not just in structure, but in spirit. Because leadership isn't defined by hierarchy it's defined by trust. It's the kind of trust that grows in your absence, not just your presence.

I don't simply build businesses. I shape cultures, one conversation, one handshake, and one moment of recognition at a time. Each decision is guided by a belief that every individual deserves to be seen, heard, and valued. This isn't just how I operate. It's who I am. It's the core of what I'll leave behind.

At home, those same values live on. Laura and I never aimed for perfection, but we stood our ground in faith, presence, and willingness to learn. We raised our children on sacred rhythms handed down to us: Sunday mornings in church, love expressed through meals, respect earned and given, hard work honored, and fear answered with faith.

If asked how I want to be remembered, it wouldn't be for profit margins or market share. I hope to be remembered for the quiet things the steady presence, the tough conversations I didn't walk away from, the hands I held when it mattered most. I want to be known for choosing grace when pride would have been easier and for believing in people when they couldn't yet believe in themselves.

Because I know firsthand what second chances can do. In business, in faith, and in family, they are not resets. They are revolutions. I have seen people change. I have changed. And that, more than any accolade, is the legacy I carry forward.

When I imagine the final chapter of my life, I don't see crowds or accolades. I see a long table that calls to mind our Sunday family dinners, wine flowing, bread torn and passed, voices overlapping in laughter and reflection. There's teasing and tenderness. Someone's eyes well up. Candlelight flickers softly, casting its familiar glow as time slows to something sacred.

This is how I wish to be remembered. As a man who honored the name he carried. A man who welcomed both joy and sorrow, who lived with humor and humility, and who handed down what he learned not with pride but with reverence.

Legacy isn't just about what we hold onto. It's about what we release. It's the imprint we leave behind in the lives of those who come next.

Nowhere is this more evident than in my oldest son, Louis J. Basenese III. In him, I see the best parts of those who came before him: a strong moral compass, a sharp mind, and a quiet strength that commands without needing to control. With Christina by his side and their four beautiful children, he has built a life rooted in integrity and grace.

Every time I see him share insight on Fox Business or Fox News, I'm struck by how he makes complex ideas feel accessible, not by simplifying the message but by respecting the intelligence of those listening. That's not just effective communication; that's leadership.

What moves me most about Lou isn't what he's achieved, though his accomplishments are considerable. It's the man he's chosen to become: a husband who shows up, a father who listens, a professional who leads with care. He has taken our family name and carried it forward not just with success but with intention.

When I watch Lou with his children, I understand that the story doesn't end with me. It continues through them. What I hope to leave behind isn't a spotless record or flawless reputation. I hope to leave behind the conviction that a meaningful life is built through humility, perseverance, and faith.

The wisdom we pass on should reflect the truth of our lives, not perfection, but redemption. Not applause, but endurance. Not wealth, but love that outlasts us.

In the end, our story was never about singular achievements. It's always been about the quiet strength of family, the kind passed down in rituals, reinforced in struggle, and carried forward in love. Our legacy was never meant to end with us; it was always meant to begin again.

Epilogue

"What Remains, What Matters"

Within these pages lies a story that extends far beyond my own. This memoir is a heartfelt tribute, a letter of thanks to those who shaped me, supported me, and walked with me through life's most challenging moments. It stands as a testament to the unwavering love and devotion of my family, both past and present. It is also a reflection of the faith that guided me and the future that continues to unfold through my children and grandchildren.

Every family carries its share of secrets, silence, and scars. What matters isn't only what we inherit. It's what we choose to heal. What began as a tribute became something more: a path toward reconciliation, an invitation to extend grace where it hadn't always been given, and a chance to leave behind something that might help someone else find their voice.

If even one reader finishes this book feeling less alone, more courageous, or more grounded, then it wasn't just a book it was a blessing.

This memoir is also a love letter to Netcong, New Jersey, the town that gave shape to my earliest memories, anchored my values, and nurtured friendships that have stood the test of time. Netcong was not just a location. It was a beginning, a proving ground, and, more than anything, a home. Its spirit has stayed with me long after the doors of Netcong High School closed in 1974.

To honor that spirit, I've made it a tradition to organize a Homecoming every year on the Sunday following the Feast of the Assumption. But this celebration is far from a solo effort. It exists because of seven extraordinary women, each of whom carries the history, strength, and heart of our town in everything they do:

Gayle Pierson (Class of 1961)

Dayle Pierson (Class of 1961)

Annette Lamberto Oswald (Class of 1965)

Ruthie Wilcock Stewart (Class of 1965)

Cindy Agens McAvoy (Class of 1967)

Marion O'Brien Fucito (Class of 1967)

Olive O'Brien Carbonaro (Class of 1968)

These remarkable women give their time, energy, and hearts to ensure the success of our Homecoming. They are pillars of strength steadfast even in the face of adversity and their efforts have made not only this book but our entire town richer in spirit and meaning.

To the entire Netcong High School alumni family, I offer my deepest gratitude. Thank you for keeping the soul of our small but mighty school alive through your memories, your hugs, and the simple, profound act of returning home.

If there is one lesson, I hope you carry with you from these pages, let it be this:

Show up for the people and the moments that matter.

Love fiercely, without hesitation or apology.

Lead with grace, humility, and compassion.

And leave behind a legacy that stretches far beyond your name.

That is the secret to a life well-lived. That is the thread of our shared connection.

And that that is the very essence of why we are here.

That's the sauce.

That's the stars.

And that...

That is heaven.

My Family Legacy

Photo Gallery

Lou & Laura — Spiritual partners,
steady through the storms of life

Three Generations of Love — Lou, Lou III and Lou IV
A bond that transcends time

Chris with Brother Lou — A brotherhood that lives

*We are Family — Maxie, Frankie, Eva Grace,
Louie, Reagan, Lou & LJ*

Fenway Park Fun — Lou IV, Reagan, Lou III & Eva Grace

Christina, Grayson, Lou III

Sisters Ruth & Bev
A lifetime of shared moments

Family Tree

"Branches of Love: The Roots that Shape Us"

Root Generation

Gabriel Basenese (b. 1888, Carpino, Italy → Netcong 1907)
married Donata Amendola (arr. 1910)

Faith-filled patriots who traded a $12 steamship ticket for a
hillside porch overlooking Lake Musconetcong.

Their Eleven Children (Birth Order*)

Birth Order	Name & Nickname	Snapshot
1	Domenick	Quiet anchor of the clan.
2	Louie (1918 – 1973) m. Eva Granato. One of the 7 Granato siblings, including Ralph†	WWII Army → Navy; butcher; policeman; my father.
3	Joseph – "Uncle Pat"	Career Navy man; discipline personified.

4	Raffaello – "Falieu"	Gentle soul, softest heart of the brothers.
5	Frank – "Uncle Stacky"	Excavation-company owner; lost in site accident.
6	Anna	4'6" lioness; mother of Paulie; fiercest defender alive.
7	Mike – "Slapsie Maxie"	Teacher turned entrepreneur; pool-hall legend.
8	Anthony	Family peacekeeper, voice of reason.
9	Mary	The family's quiet matriarchal power broker.
10	Angelo – "Rogue in the Room"	Swagger, pranks, $500 porch pickpocket; died at 38.
11	Pasquale - Patsy	Used-car dealer with the gift of the hustle.

Children:

Ruth	The wise eldest.
Beverly	Unstoppable compassion.
Lou, Jr. (author)	Entrepreneur & narrator of this memoir.

Grandchildren through Lou, Jr.:

Louis J. Basenese III	Financial journalist; married Christina; four children.
Christopher Neal Basenese (1980–2019)	skateboarder, free spirit; memorialized in "Last Kiss" photo.

Great Grandchildren through Lou III:

Four beloved children, continuing the legacy of faith, family, and love into a new generation

Notable Next-Gen Cousins

Paulie (Anna's son):	Charm & loyalty mentored by Angelo.
Mike Leavy:	Boyhood best friend "who shared everything."
Frankie (Stacky's son):	Dover football star; living embodiment of Netcong grit.
Maxie, Jr.:	White-leisure-suit legend turned devoted family man.

Who's Who

Around the Sunday Table

"Colorful Characters breathing Life into the Story"

Lou Basenese (Author)

As the son of Louie and Eva, I was born and raised in Netcong alongside my two older sisters, Ruth and Beverly. Together, we formed a tight-knit family rooted in faith, hard work, and tradition. These values shaped my heart and steadied my path through life's storms through redemption in Christ, victories earned through adversity, and the restorative power of family.

Ruth, the eldest, has always been a beacon of wisdom and quiet strength. Beverly brings an unstoppable spirit and boundless compassion. Each of them has added a distinct thread to the tapestry of our family's legacy, and I am grateful for the journey we've shared.

As a devoted husband, loving father, ambitious entrepreneur, storyteller, and spiritual leader, I strive to honor the past while preparing the next generation to carry our name with resilience and grace. Together, we continue the work of building a legacy of love.

Gabriel & Donata (Paternal Grandparents)

My paternal grandparents, Gabriel and Donata, were the foundation on which so much of our family was built. Gabriel, an Italian immigrant who passed through Ellis Island and endured more name changes than we could count, embodied the courage of a generation willing to risk everything for a better life. Beside him stood Donata, unyielding, devoted, and quietly powerful.

Together, they transplanted the rich soul of Southern Italy to a modest porch overlooking Lake Musconetcong. Their Sunday tables weren't just meals they were rituals of togetherness, full of pasta, prayer, and purpose. Their legacy is alive in every family gathering, in every shared laugh and candlelit story. Their love lives on.

Nanna (Eva's Mother)

Nanna, the matriarch of Port Morris, was part saint, part sorceress. Her front porch was a spiritual haven adorned with prayer candles, holy statues, and the quiet mystery of old-world rituals.

She walked the line between sacred and superstitious, wielding her wisdom with both tenderness and authority. Her blessings could lift you; her judgments could shake you. Nanna didn't just practice faith. She embodied it. Her presence was unforgettable, a living bridge between ancient roots and modern lives. To this day, she reminds us of the mystical depth woven into our family's cultural soul.

Immediate Family

Louie & Eva

Louie and Eva anchored the Basenese home with a blend of grit, duty, and fierce devotion. Louie, hardened by service in World War II and a career as butcher and a special police officer for the town of Netcong, carried the burden of protector and provider with a quiet determination. He was a man of rules and sharp expectations, but beneath that exterior lived a devotion to his family that never faltered. His love showed itself not through grand gestures but in his presence, his work ethic, and his enduring sense of responsibility.

Eva, his partner in all things, embodied a different kind of strength. Graceful and emotionally layered, she brought warmth and culture to the household, yet she bore the scars of hardship that left her both tender and guarded. Her resilience was forged in silence, seen not in words but in the way she set the table, corrected a child, or stood her ground when life pressed too hard. The marriage of Louie and Eva was never performative. It was lived deeply, daily, through acts of service, shared faith, and the kind of love that survives by choice as much as by emotion. Their legacy remains visible in every small act passed down: the rituals of Sunday dinners, the instinct to show up for others, and the lessons of love taught through endurance.

Christopher

Christopher, Lou's beloved son, moved through life with a rare kind of grace that was both grounded and untamed. A skateboarder with a deep soul, he was as comfortable navigating the streets as he was writing his thoughts with the clarity of someone far older than his years. He didn't need to declare who he was. He simply lived it fully and freely.

His death, caused by fentanyl poisoning, struck the family with a grief too wide for words. But even in loss, Christopher's spirit remains vivid. His 2004 letter, discovered and cherished, has become a touchstone for understanding the depth of his heart, a document that now carries weight far beyond paper. He is remembered not only for what was taken but for what he gave in his short time: honesty, wonder, and a kind of emotional fluency that left its mark on everyone who knew him.

Laura

Laura, Lou's wife and spiritual counterpart, holds a space in this story that is quiet but mighty. Through seasons of illness, mourning, and renewal, she has remained steady, offering her strength not through declarations but through constancy. Her presence is one of quiet faith, shaped by a trust in things beyond the visible, and her capacity for love has carried Lou through his most difficult chapters.

She is the kind of woman whose strength shows in the way she listens, in how she prays, and in the unshakable kindness she extends when others are too weary to continue. More than a partner, she has been Lou's witness, protector, and fellow traveler, someone who walks beside him not only in ease but in every valley, every waiting room, every long night. Her influence is not just spiritual; it's structural. She is part of what has held this family together, even when the winds tried to pull them apart.

Aunt Anna

Aunt Anna stood just 4'6", but her presence filled every room. Her stature was small, yet her spirit was formidable, protective, unwavering, and fierce in her devotion. Her eyes could quiet a room before she spoke a word, and when tensions rose, her stare alone was enough to restore order. She moved through the world with the energy of a lioness, never needing to raise her voice to command respect. Her love ran hot and immediate, while her anger struck like a sudden storm when someone she cared about was threatened. In a family filled with strong personalities, Aunt Anna stood firm, unyielding in her loyalty and love. She was the kind of woman whose strength wasn't loud but lasting, and she remains one of the most enduring pillars in our collective memory.

Angelo

Angelo was the family's spark: reckless, magnetic, and unforgettable. He wasn't merely a brother or an uncle; he was a myth wrapped in flesh, full of stories that walked the line between wild and wonderful. With a glint in his eye, he could lift $500 from his brother's coat one moment and offer heartfelt wisdom the next. He lived out loud with a charm that disarmed and mischief that never quite apologized. Angelo's bond with Paulie extended beyond uncle and nephew; it was a partnership of spirit, a sharing of stories, lessons, and laughter that shaped them both. To Louie, Angelo could be maddening, a live wire that never grounded, but even then, love threaded through the frustration. His time was brief, but his legacy was boundless, carried in the humor, recklessness, and love that still ripple through every family gathering.

Paulie

Paulie, son of Aunt Anna and nephew to Angelo, carried the best of both within him. Charismatic and sharp, he inherited Anna's loyalty and Angelo's charm. He was one of those rare souls who never had to raise his voice to be heard or do much to be remembered. There was wisdom behind his humor and depth behind his smile, and when he entered a room, people instinctively leaned closer. Angelo mentored him not just in mischief but in character, teaching by example through both the good and the flawed. Paulie lived in a way that felt true to the Basenese name: fiercely loyal, deeply rooted in family, and full of a quiet, consistent love that never asked for attention but always gave it.

Mike Leavy

Mike Leavy was more than a best friend, he was the kind of person you trust with your silence. From their earliest days, Mike and Lou shared a brotherhood that never needed explanation. Their friendship began in the innocence of boyhood games but deepened into something sacred as the years added trials and milestones. Through every turn, Mike remained at Lou's side not just a witness to life, but a participant in its hardest and brightest chapters. He wasn't bound by blood but by choice and constancy, and that made him family in the truest sense. His presence in Lou's life is a reminder that not all kin are born. Some are chosen, and those bonds can be even stronger.

Frankie

Frankie taught me that family doesn't always come from proximity. It lives in the way someone shows up, speaks the truth, and keeps showing up even when it's hard. He wasn't just a cousin; he was a mirror to our family's resilience, a living echo of strength shaped by grit and humility. Whether near or far, Frankie's actions proved that love is measured less by frequency and more by loyalty. In a world that moves fast and forgets often, Frankie never did. His quiet presence left a lasting mark, not by what he said but by the kind of man he chose to be.

Maxie

Maxie entered every room like sunlight through a window—warm, effortless, unmistakable. He didn't announce himself with grand speeches or demand to be seen; he simply *was*, and that was enough. His energy didn't ask permission to exist. It spilled into the corners, lifted moods, and wrapped itself around people like a familiar song you didn't know you missed until you heard it again. Laughter followed him naturally, like a shadow in reverse, and ease seemed to bloom wherever he stood.

People didn't gravitate toward Maxie because he sought attention. They were drawn to him because he embodied something rare—unfiltered joy. The kind that made you feel lighter just being near it. The kind that said, *It's okay to breathe here. It's okay to laugh. It's okay to let go for a moment.*

And yet, behind the magnetism was a story not everyone saw right away. His charm wasn't the product of an easy life—it was the reward of a hard-won one. Maxie's journey wasn't neat or linear. There were detours and setbacks, heartbreaks and healing, choices he laughed about later and a few he carried quietly. But through it all, he never lost his sense of self. He adapted, evolved, and reinvented—but always in a way that was uniquely *him*.

Sometimes that reinvention came wrapped in a cream white leisure suit, topped with a grin and sunglasses no one else could pull off. Maxie made flair into a language. He knew how to turn pain into punchlines, missteps into dance moves, and ordinary moments into lasting memories. His life reminded us that healing doesn't always look solemn—it can wear a smile, tell a joke, and turn up the music.

He taught us that family is not about perfection, but about presence. That loving someone means honoring every layer of who they are—past, present, and becoming. Maxie never denied the messy parts. He danced with them. He dressed them up. He welcomed them to the table and poured them a drink.

At every family gathering, his stories were the ones we waited for—not just because they were funny or wild (though they often were), but because they made us feel seen. Underneath the laughter was always a thread of truth— a reminder that joy can be defiant, that resilience doesn't have to wear a frown, and that the strongest people often carry the light for others even when their own path gets dark.

To know Maxie was to know that love could be loud. That warmth could be wild. That legacy isn't built on awards or titles—it's built on the moments when someone makes you feel like you belong, just by being themselves.

And Maxie? He did that every time he walked into a room.

Vincent "Harvey" Togno

Vincent Togno, affectionately known as "Harvey," was more than a Marine and an educator. He was a pillar of influence for countless young people. As a Physical Education and Health teacher, he brought the discipline of the Corps into the classroom, balanced with a genuine care for his students' well-being. His nickname reflected the unique duality of his nature: firm but compassionate, exacting yet encouraging. Harvey believed in the potential of every student who walked through his doors. He didn't just teach lessons; he instilled values. His impact remains etched in the lives of those he guided, a steady presence that continues to shape his character long after graduation.

Gus Rampone

Coach Gus Rampone was the embodiment of conviction and integrity. As both an educator and head football coach, he pushed his students to exceed their limits not through intimidation but through belief in what they could become. He had the rare ability to make young people feel seen and capable, and it was that fierce belief that often became the difference between self-doubt and self-discovery. His leadership left its mark not only on the playing field but on the hearts of those he mentored. The confidence he instilled in us didn't fade with time; it became a part of who we are.

Carmine "Mo" DeMuccio

Carmine DeMuccio, known to most as "Mo," had a presence that demanded respect but offered far more than authority. His approach was structured, his expectations high, and his tone unwavering. Yet beneath that discipline was a deep well of care. He saw strength in his students even when they didn't see it in themselves. Mo's mentorship was never just about discipline it was about unlocking the quiet resilience in every young person who crossed his path. His influence went far beyond the locker room or the classroom. It showed up years later in the choices we made, in the strength we leaned on, and in the lives, we tried to live with honor.

Netcong

Netcong was never just a dot on a map. It was and remains a heartbeat, its rhythm deeply familiar to those of us who grew up within its embrace. Nestled in the folds of Morris County, this close-knit Italian-American community stood as a constant, where faith was practiced, loyalty was lived, and family was everything. Its narrow streets held the echoes of a thousand family dinners, front porch conversations, and Sunday Masses. For the Basenese family, Netcong offered more than shelter. It offered identity. It shaped us in ways both subtle and profound, becoming the quiet force that underpinned our values and our view of the world. Here, celebrations felt fuller, losses found support, and time seemed to move in step with memory. Netcong is not just where we live; it's part of who we are.

Our Family's Journey

From the Hills of Italy to New Jersey

Our story begins in Carpino, a hillside village in southern Italy where tradition ran deep, and family was the cornerstone of life. It was there that Gabriel Bassanise and Donata Amendola planted the first roots of what would grow into a multigenerational legacy, one shaped by faith, perseverance, and unyielding love. Their journey carried them from those ancestral hills to the quiet neighborhoods of Netcong, New Jersey, where their values took root in new soil, nurturing not only their eleven children, including my parents Louie and Eva but also every generation that followed.

As we trace our path across continents and decades, we find that some things remain untouched by time. Names may change. Homes may rise and fall. But the essence, the sauce that binds us together, remains constant. It is the steady beat of shared meals, the passed-down prayers, the laughter, the loss, and the grit that define who we are.

This memoir is a tribute to those who came before us, those whose sacrifices shaped our comforts, and whose dreams became our starting point. It is my sincere hope that in these pages, our children and grandchildren will discover not only where they came from but also why they matter and that they carry within them the same strength, humor, and heart that guided us.

May our family's journey, from the hills of Italy to the streets of New Jersey, serve as a beacon to anyone seeking meaning in their roots. And may our legacy live on, not just in memory, but in the lives, we continue to build, love by love, choice by choice.

Final Blessing

In God's Hands
"A Blessing Rooted in Trust and Surrender"

As this memoir comes to a close, I offer a blessing that has endured through generations: a prayer of trust, surrender, and the quiet certainty of faith. May these words serve as a lamp for your journey, a reminder that the path ahead is not meant to be walked alone.

In a world that often urges us to lean on our strength and understanding, may you instead find peace in trusting the Lord with your whole heart. In every decision, in every uncertainty, may you seek His wisdom and yield to His guidance, for it is through this surrender that you will uncover a path that is steady, purposeful, and filled with grace.

Let the timeless words of Proverbs 3:5–6 be written not only on these pages but also on the walls of your heart:

"Trust in the Lord with all your heart

and lean not on your own understanding;

in all your ways submit to him,

and he will make your paths straight."

May this promise remain with you wherever life leads. And may your steps be ordered by a faith that does not waver, even when the road is unclear.

May you always walk forward with peace, knowing that your life, like this story, is held in hands far greater than our own.

About The Author

Grit, Grace, and the Tenacious Spirit
"The Lou Basenese Story"

Meet Lou Basenese, husband, father, entrepreneur, and storyteller. His life is grounded in faith, shaped by family, and marked by the enduring strength of small-town Italian-American heritage. Through perseverance and purpose, Lou has forged a path defined not only by professional success but by the personal integrity that underpins it.

His journey has taken him across peaks of corporate leadership and valleys of profound loss. From a near-death experience that transformed his outlook to the quiet moments of healing that followed, Lou's life is a testament to resilience in the face of the unimaginable. Professionally, he has led divisions of Fortune 500 companies, built nationally recognized consumer brands, and co-founded a successful woman-owned business. Yet his greatest accomplishments are those of character rooted in love, courage, and conviction.

With each challenge, Lou has chosen not bitterness but belief. Excuses never held sway in his world only a forward motion born of passion, persistence, and faith. His story reminds us that true grit is not about surviving the storm but rising within it, choosing each day to walk forward with heart and humility.

Between the Sauce, Stars, and Heaven is Lou's first memoir, a tribute to his roots, a reflection on who he has become, and a celebration of the faith that carried him through. His words extend an invitation to reflect on your own story, to find strength in grace, and to write each new chapter with courage and clarity.